SPIDER-MAN
SPIDER-WOMEN

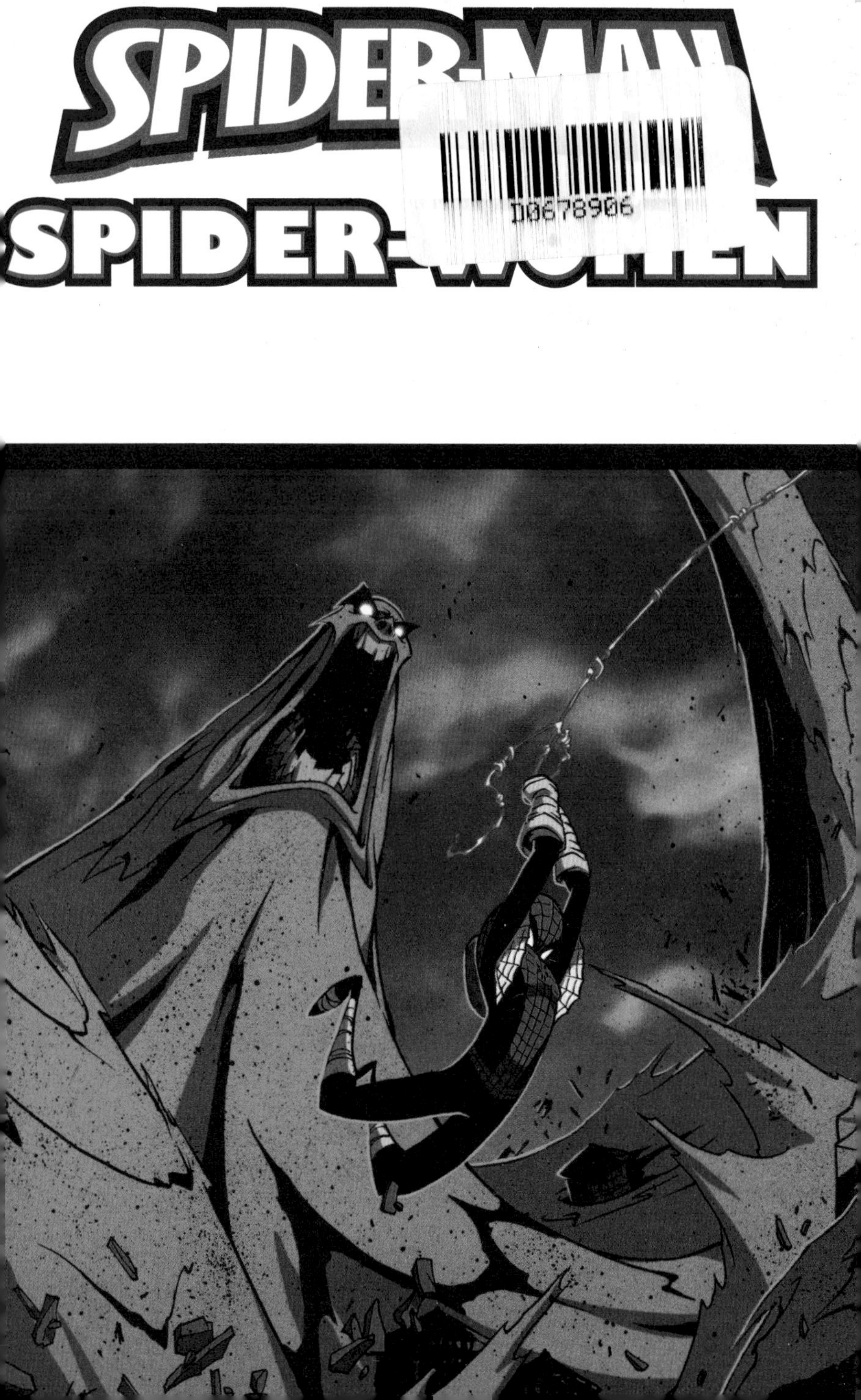

SPIDER-MAN
SPIDER-WOMEN

"UN-ENCHANTED EVENING"
Writer: Paul Tobin
Artist: Colleen Coover

"OLD ENEMIES NEVER DIE"
Script, Plot & Pencils: Tom DeFalco & Ron Lim
Inker: Norm Rapmund
Colors: Avalon Studios' Rob Ro
Letters: Dave Sharpe
Editor: Molly Lazer

"THE DANCE"
Writer: Tom DeFalco
Penciler: Ron Lim
Inker: Scott Koblish
Colors: Avalon Studios' Rob Ro
Editor: Molly Lazer

"ELEMENTAL EVIL "
Writer: C.B. Cebulski
Artist: Skottie Young
Colors: Skottie Young
& Jean-Francois Beaulieu
Letters: Virtual Calligraphy's
Randy Gentile
Editor: John Barber

Collection Editor: Cory Levine
Editorial Assistant: Alex Starbuck
Assistant Editor: John Denning
Editors, Special Projects:
Jennifer Grünwald & Mark D. Beazley
Senior Editor, Special Projects: Jeff Youngquist
Senior Vice President of Sales: David Gabriel
Production: Jerry Kalinowski

Editor in Chief: Joe Quesada
Publisher: Dan Buckley
Executive Producer: Alan Fine

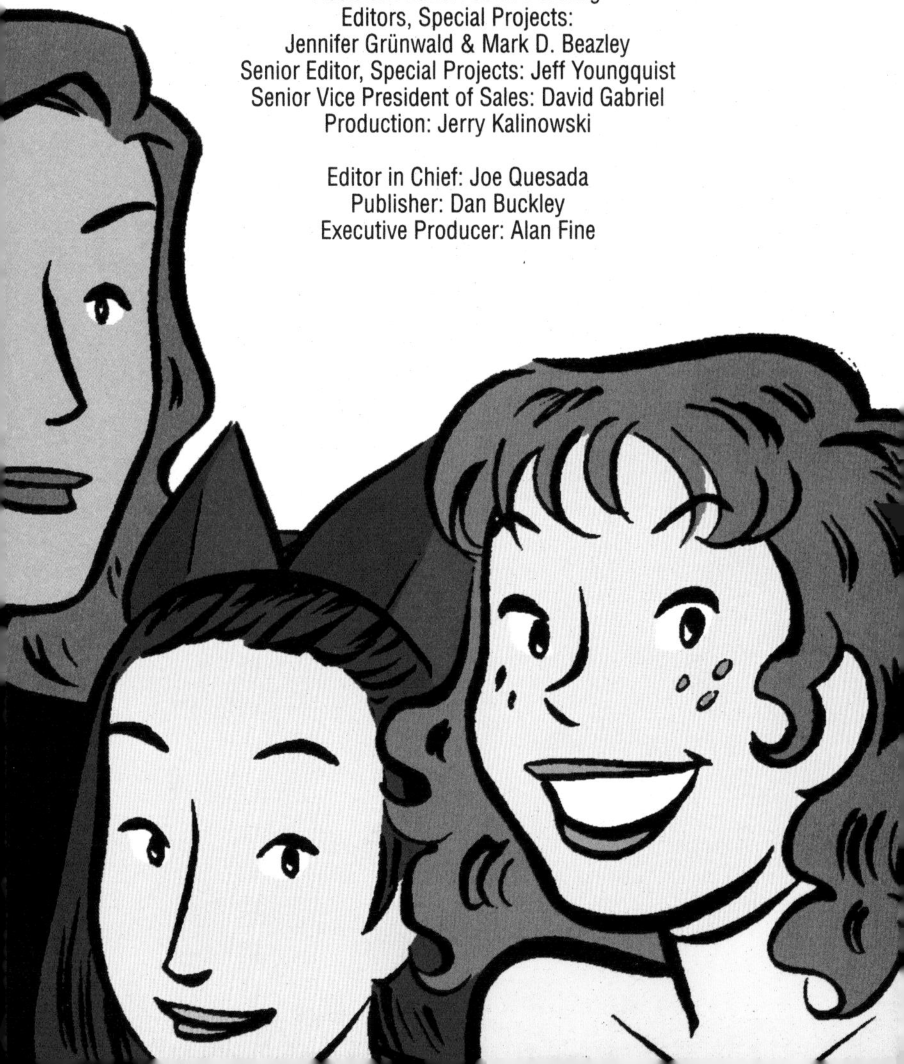

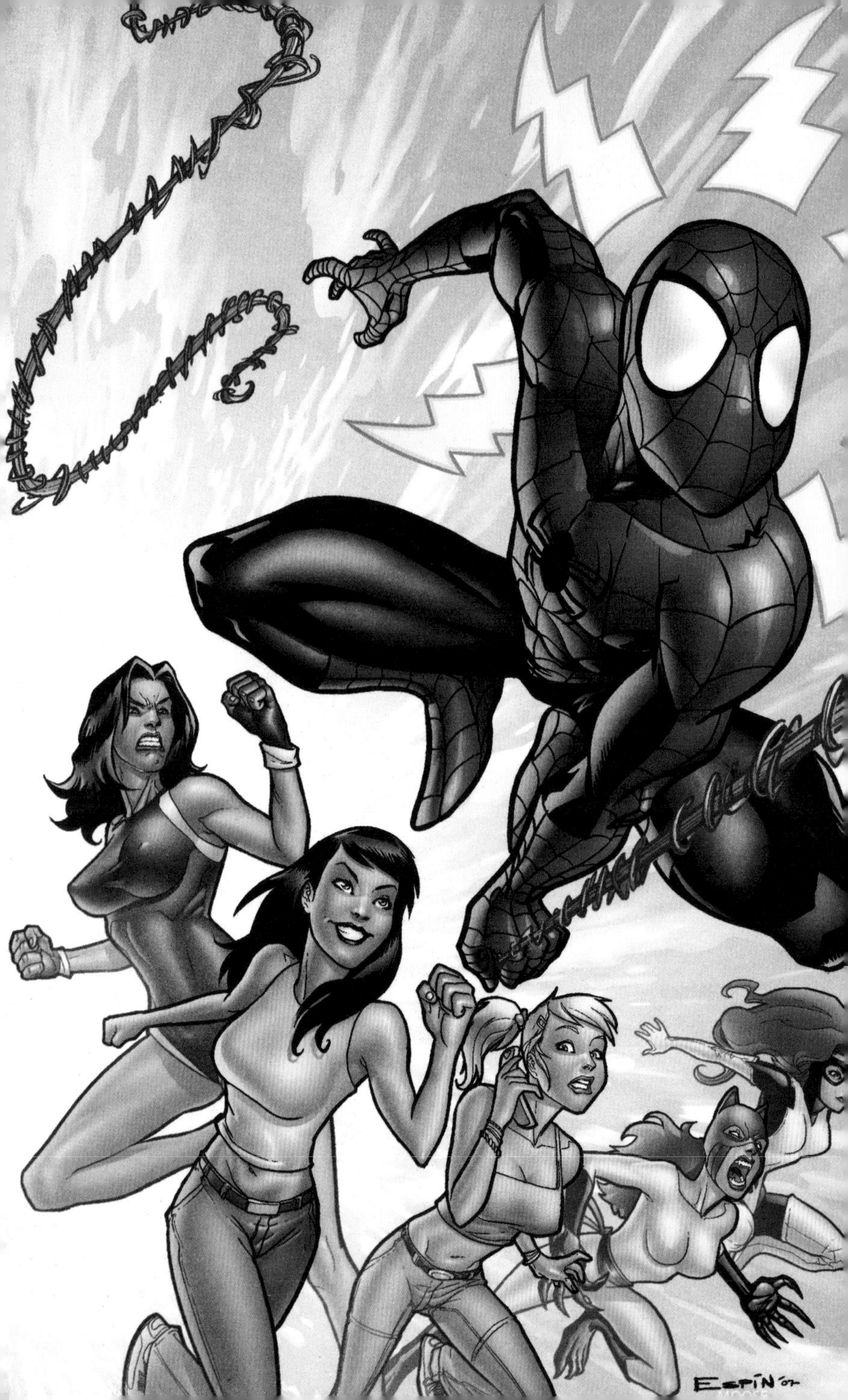
ESPIN '07

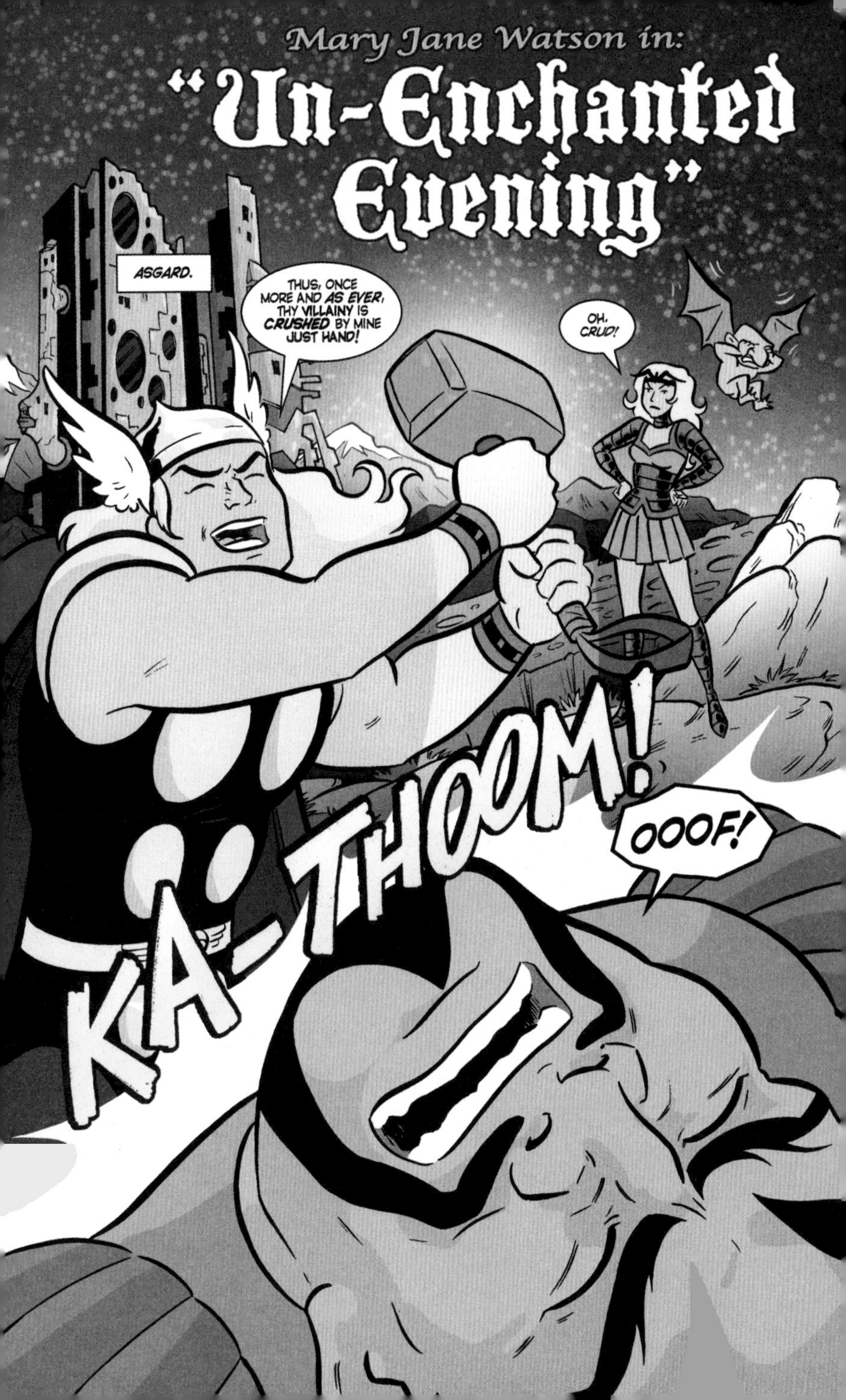
Mary Jane Watson in:
"Un-Enchanted Evening"
ASGARD.
THUS, ONCE MORE AND AS EVER, THY VILLAINY IS CRUSHED BY MINE JUST HAND!
OH, CRUD!
KA-THOOM!
OOOF!

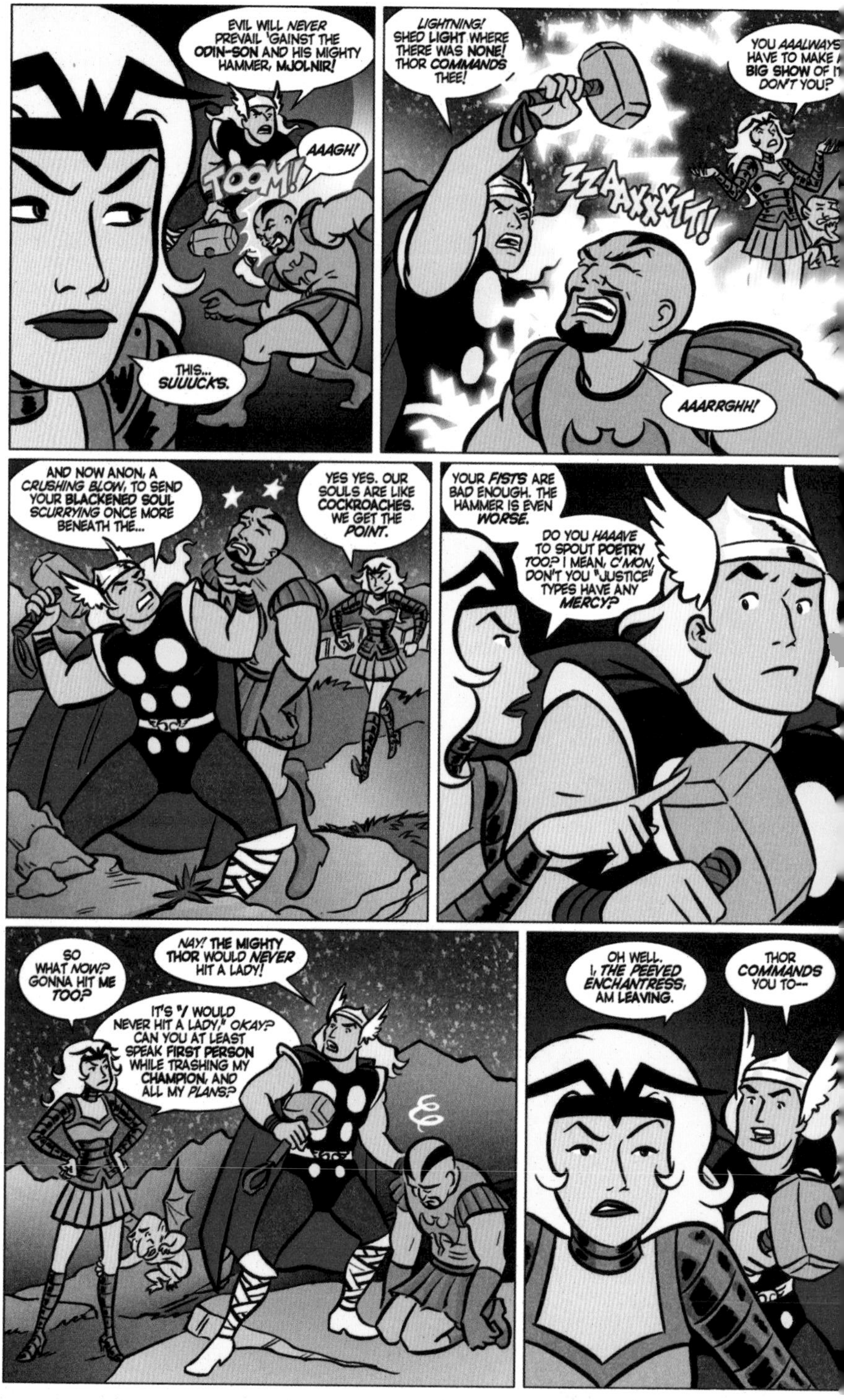
EVIL WILL NEVER PREVAIL 'GAINST THE ODIN-SON AND HIS MIGHTY HAMMER, MJOLNIR!
AAAGH!
TOOM!!
THIS... SUUUCKS.
LIGHTNING! SHED LIGHT WHERE THERE WAS NONE! THOR COMMANDS THEE!
ZZAAXXXTTT!!
YOU AAALWAYS HAVE TO MAKE BIG SHOW OF DON'T YOU?
AAARRGHH!
AND NOW ANON, A CRUSHING BLOW, TO SEND YOUR BLACKENED SOUL SCURRYING ONCE MORE BENEATH THE...
YES YES. OUR SOULS ARE LIKE COCKROACHES. WE GET THE POINT.
YOUR FISTS ARE BAD ENOUGH. THE HAMMER IS EVEN WORSE.
DO YOU HAAAVE TO SPOUT POETRY TOO? I MEAN, C'MON, DON'T YOU "JUSTICE" TYPES HAVE ANY MERCY?
SO WHAT NOW? GONNA HIT ME TOO?
NAY! THE MIGHTY THOR WOULD NEVER HIT A LADY!
IT'S "I WOULD NEVER HIT A LADY," OKAY? CAN YOU AT LEAST SPEAK FIRST PERSON WHILE TRASHING MY CHAMPION, AND ALL MY PLANS?
OH WELL. I, THE PEEVED ENCHANTRESS, AM LEAVING.
THOR COMMANDS YOU TO--

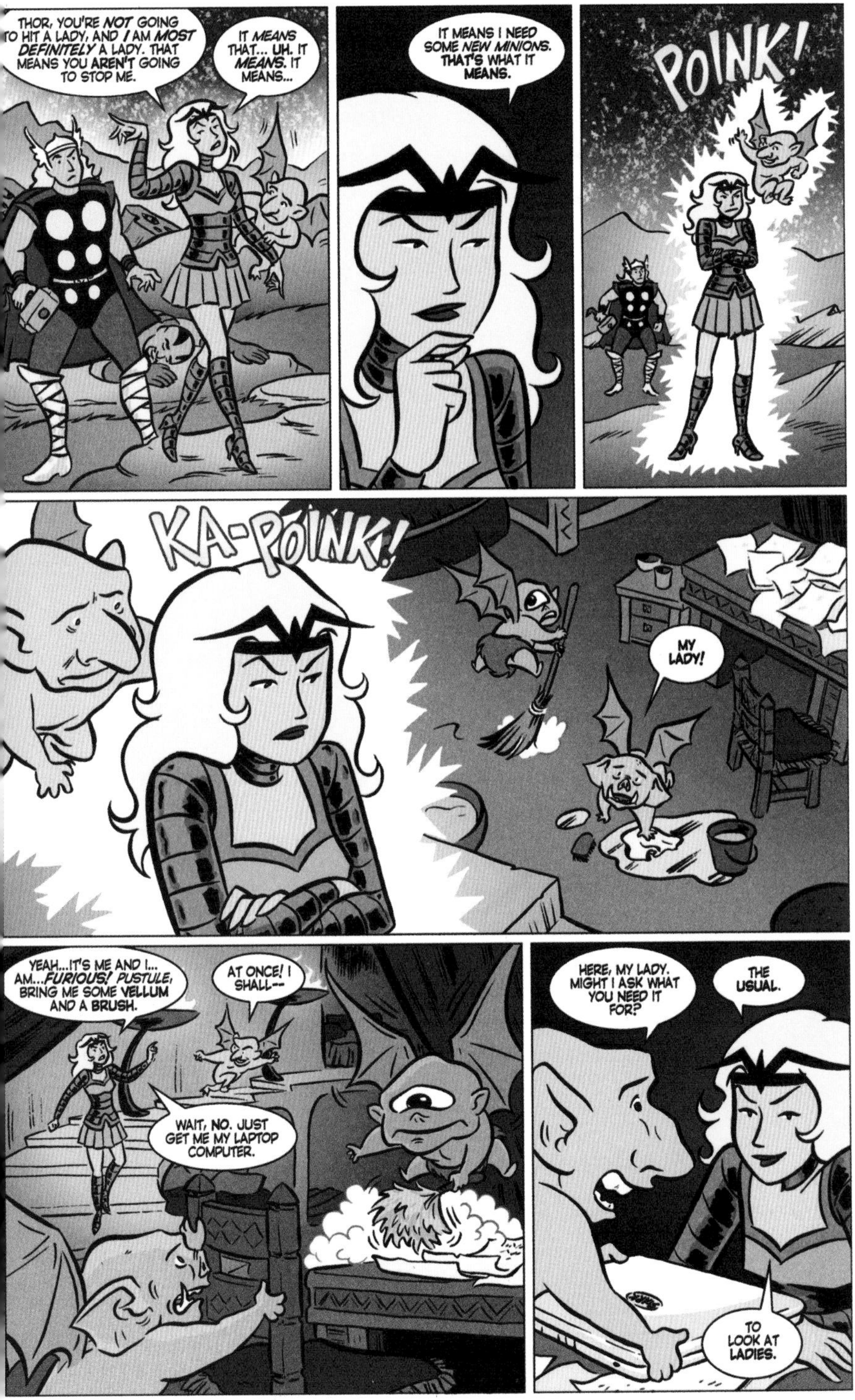
THOR, YOU'RE NOT GOING TO HIT A LADY, AND I AM MOST DEFINITELY A LADY. THAT MEANS YOU AREN'T GOING TO STOP ME.
IT MEANS THAT... UH. IT MEANS. IT MEANS...
IT MEANS I NEED SOME NEW MINIONS. THAT'S WHAT IT MEANS.
POINK!
KA-POINK!
MY LADY!
YEAH...IT'S ME AND I... AM...FURIOUS! PUSTULE, BRING ME SOME VELLUM AND A BRUSH.
AT ONCE! I SHALL--
WAIT, NO. JUST GET ME MY LAPTOP COMPUTER.
HERE, MY LADY. MIGHT I ASK WHAT YOU NEED IT FOR?
THE USUAL.
TO LOOK AT LADIES.

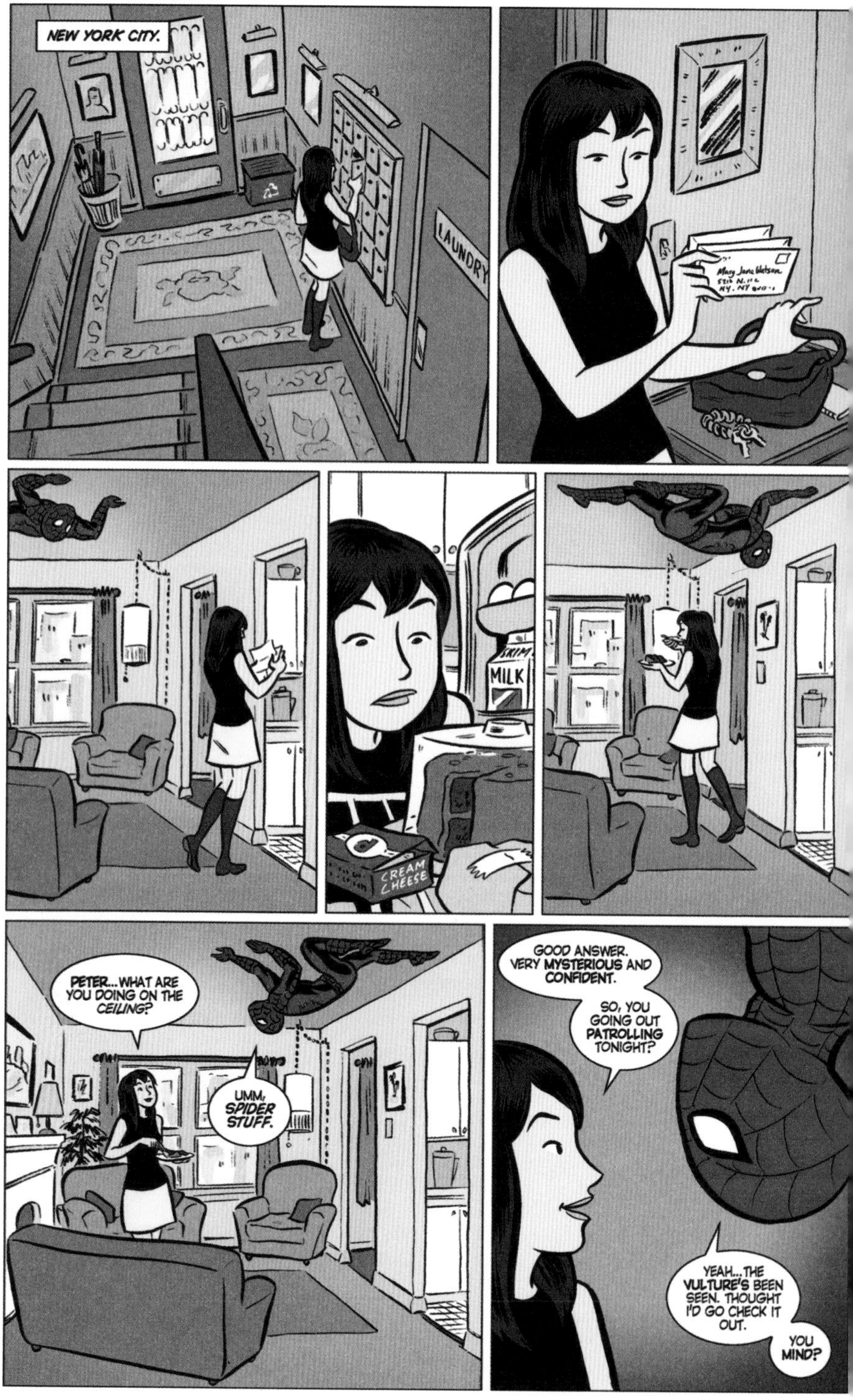
NEW YORK CITY.
LAUNDRY
Mary Jane Watson
SKIM MILK
CREAM CHEESE
PETER...WHAT ARE YOU DOING ON THE *CEILING*?
UMM, *SPIDER STUFF*.
GOOD ANSWER. VERY **MYSTERIOUS** AND **CONFIDENT**.
SO, YOU GOING OUT **PATROLLING** TONIGHT?
YEAH...THE **VULTURE'S** BEEN SEEN. THOUGHT I'D GO CHECK IT OUT.
YOU **MIND**?

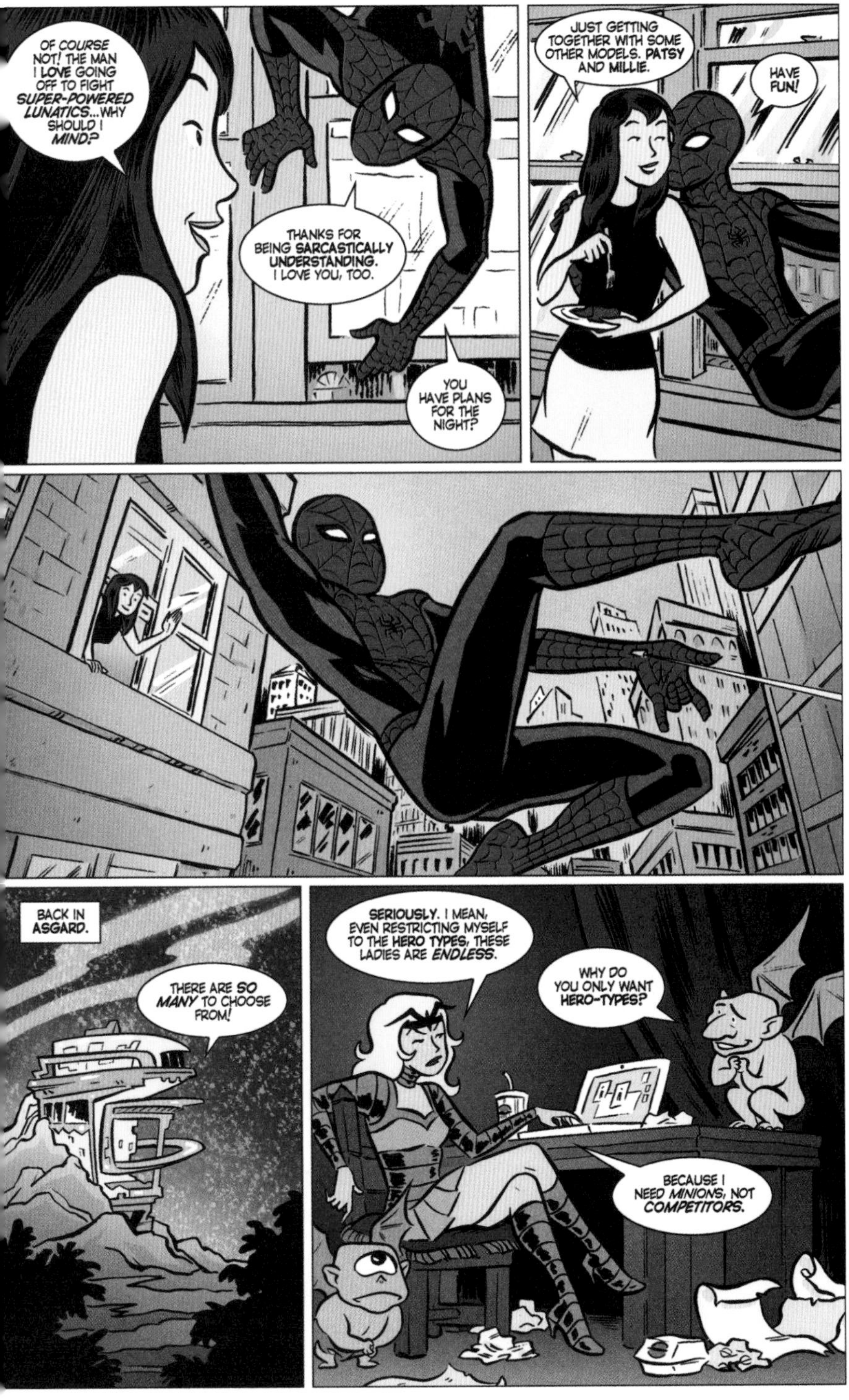
OF COURSE NOT! THE MAN I LOVE GOING OFF TO FIGHT SUPER-POWERED LUNATICS...WHY SHOULD I MIND?
THANKS FOR BEING SARCASTICALLY UNDERSTANDING. I LOVE YOU, TOO.
YOU HAVE PLANS FOR THE NIGHT?
JUST GETTING TOGETHER WITH SOME OTHER MODELS. PATSY AND MILLIE.
HAVE FUN!
BACK IN ASGARD.
THERE ARE SO MANY TO CHOOSE FROM!
SERIOUSLY. I MEAN, EVEN RESTRICTING MYSELF TO THE HERO TYPES, THESE LADIES ARE ENDLESS.
WHY DO YOU ONLY WANT HERO-TYPES?
BECAUSE I NEED MINIONS, NOT COMPETITORS.

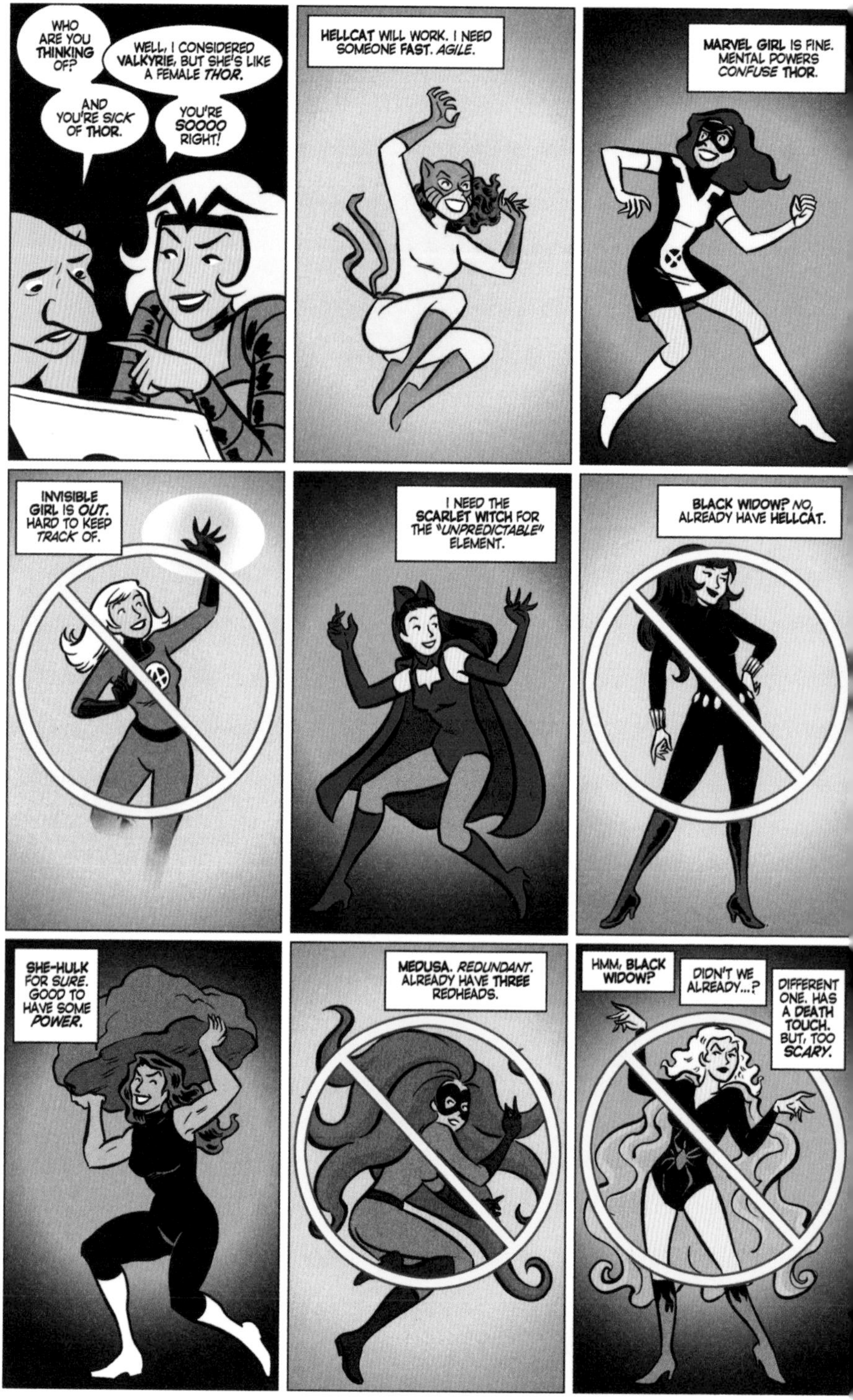
WHO ARE YOU THINKING OF?
WELL, I CONSIDERED VALKYRIE, BUT SHE'S LIKE A FEMALE THOR.
AND YOU'RE SICK OF THOR.
YOU'RE SOOOO RIGHT!
HELLCAT WILL WORK. I NEED SOMEONE FAST. AGILE.
MARVEL GIRL IS FINE. MENTAL POWERS CONFUSE THOR.
INVISIBLE GIRL IS OUT. HARD TO KEEP TRACK OF.
I NEED THE SCARLET WITCH FOR THE "UNPREDICTABLE" ELEMENT.
BLACK WIDOW? NO, ALREADY HAVE HELLCAT.
SHE-HULK FOR SURE. GOOD TO HAVE SOME POWER.
MEDUSA. REDUNDANT. ALREADY HAVE THREE REDHEADS.
HMM, BLACK WIDOW?
DIDN'T WE ALREADY...?
DIFFERENT ONE. HAS A DEATH TOUCH. BUT, TOO SCARY.

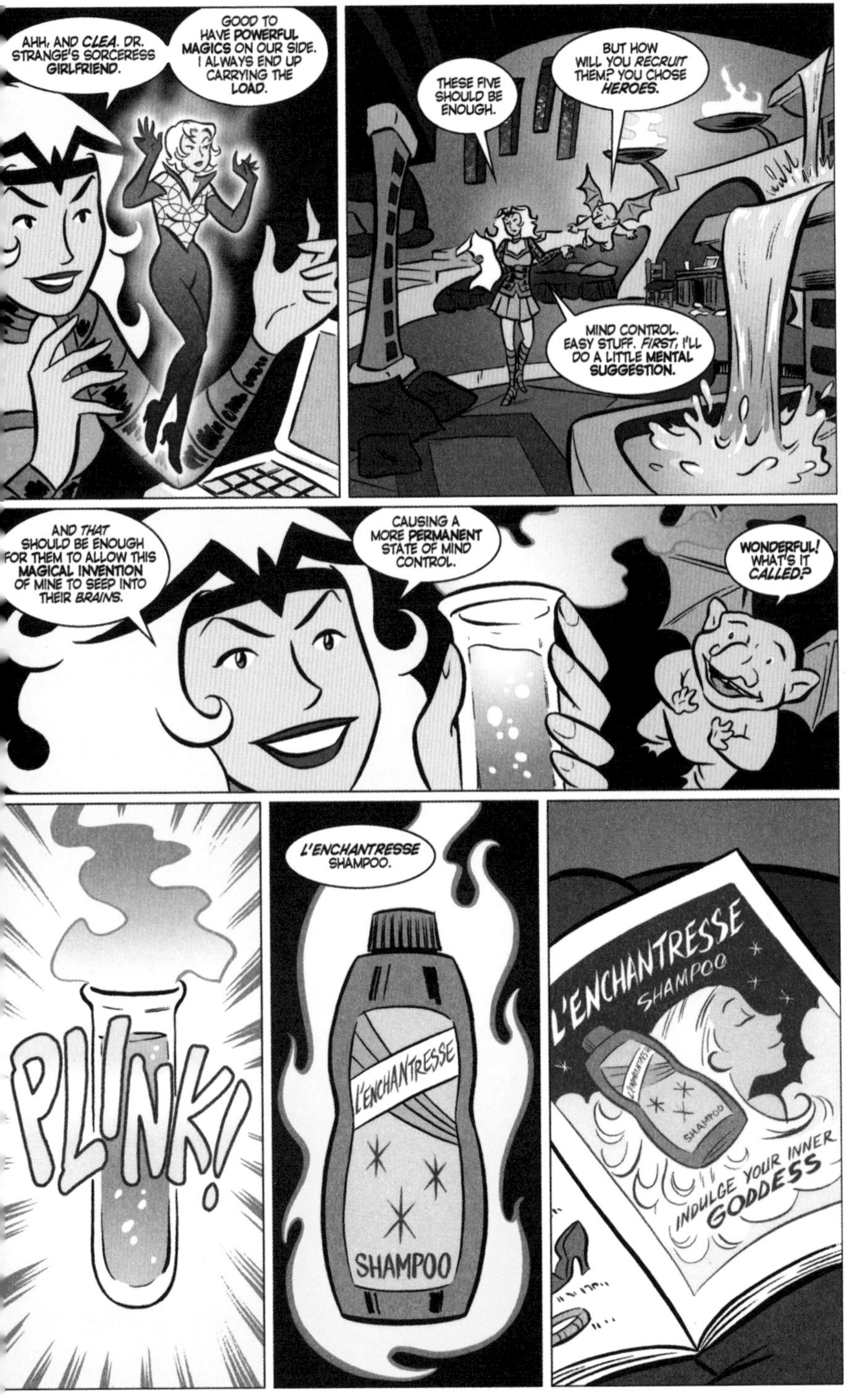
AHH, AND CLEA. DR. STRANGE'S SORCERESS GIRLFRIEND.
GOOD TO HAVE POWERFUL MAGICS ON OUR SIDE. I ALWAYS END UP CARRYING THE LOAD.
THESE FIVE SHOULD BE ENOUGH.
BUT HOW WILL YOU RECRUIT THEM? YOU CHOSE HEROES.
MIND CONTROL. EASY STUFF. FIRST, I'LL DO A LITTLE MENTAL SUGGESTION.
AND THAT SHOULD BE ENOUGH FOR THEM TO ALLOW THIS MAGICAL INVENTION OF MINE TO SEEP INTO THEIR BRAINS.
CAUSING A MORE PERMANENT STATE OF MIND CONTROL.
WONDERFUL! WHAT'S IT CALLED?
PLINK!
L'ENCHANTRESSE SHAMPOO.
L'ENCHANTRESSE
SHAMPOO
L'ENCHANTRESSE
SHAMPOO
INDULGE YOUR INNER GODDESS

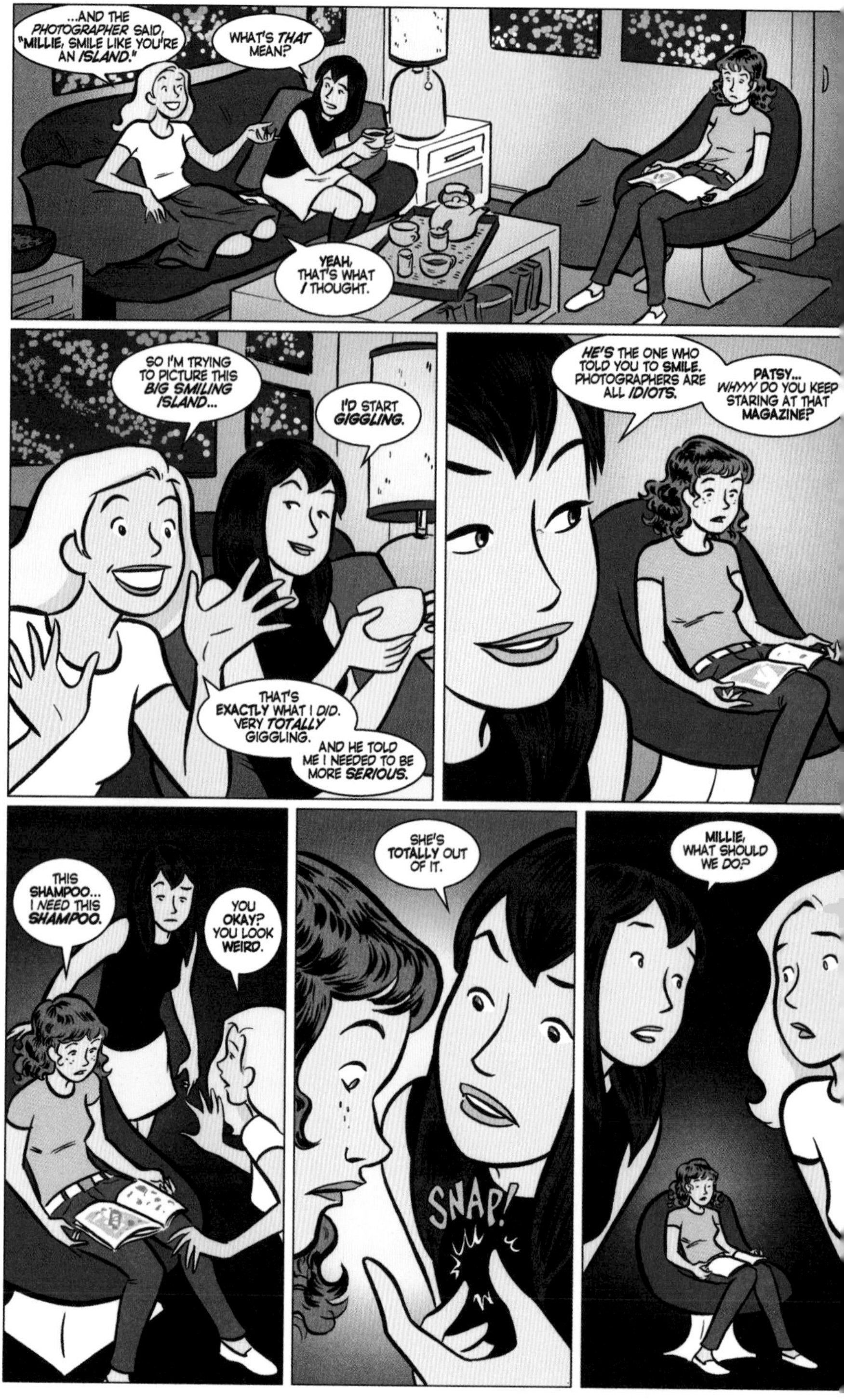
...AND THE PHOTOGRAPHER SAID, "MILLIE, SMILE LIKE YOU'RE AN ISLAND."
WHAT'S THAT MEAN?
YEAH, THAT'S WHAT I THOUGHT.
SO I'M TRYING TO PICTURE THIS BIG SMILING ISLAND...
I'D START GIGGLING.
THAT'S EXACTLY WHAT I DID. VERY TOTALLY GIGGLING.
AND HE TOLD ME I NEEDED TO BE MORE SERIOUS.
HE'S THE ONE WHO TOLD YOU TO SMILE. PHOTOGRAPHERS ARE ALL IDIOTS.
PATSY... WHYYY DO YOU KEEP STARING AT THAT MAGAZINE?
THIS SHAMPOO... I NEED THIS SHAMPOO.
YOU OKAY? YOU LOOK WEIRD.
SHE'S TOTALLY OUT OF IT.
SNAP!
MILLIE, WHAT SHOULD WE DO?

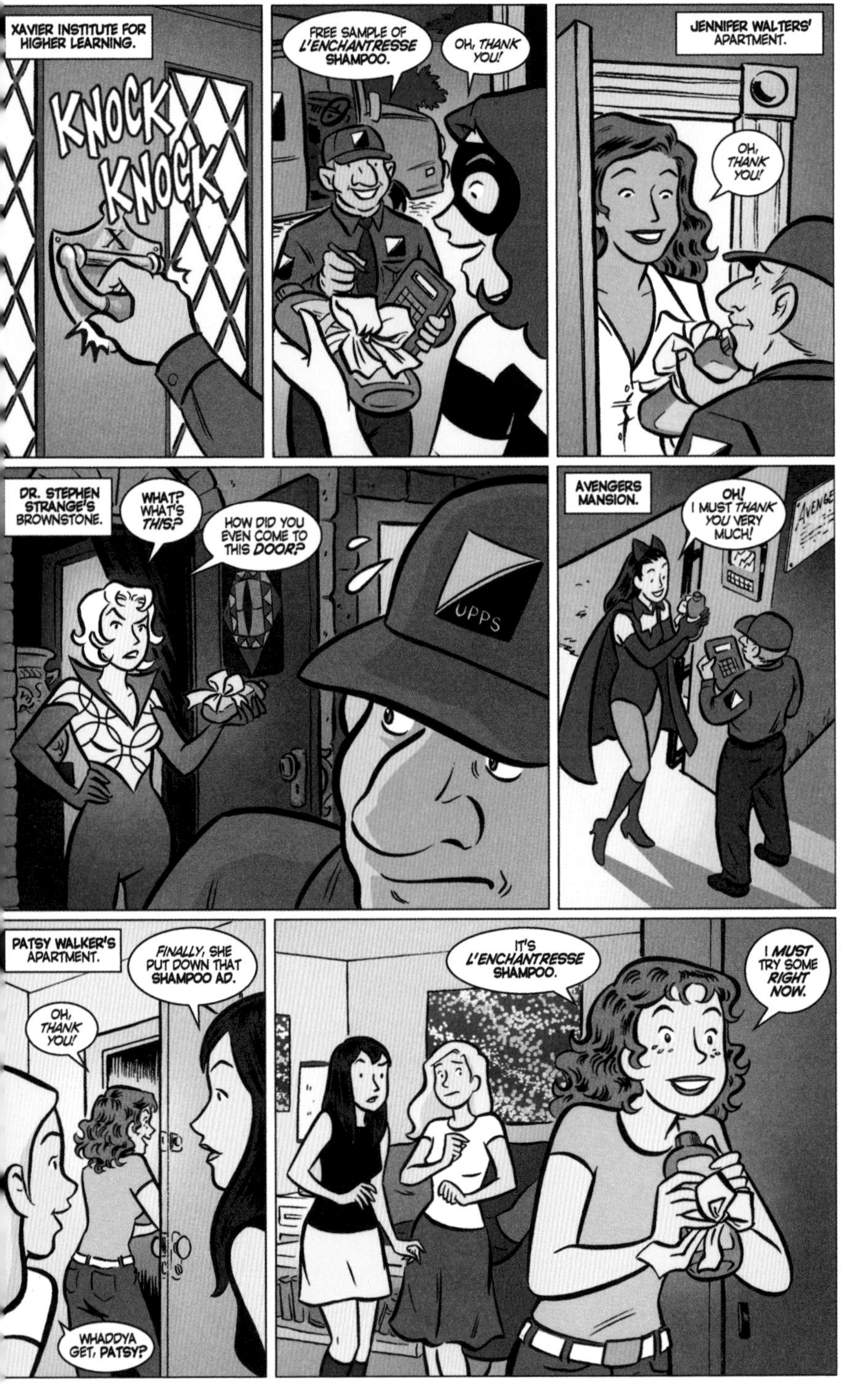
XAVIER INSTITUTE FOR HIGHER LEARNING.
KNOCK KNOCK
X
FREE SAMPLE OF L'ENCHANTRESSE SHAMPOO.
OH, THANK YOU!
JENNIFER WALTERS' APARTMENT.
OH, THANK YOU!
DR. STEPHEN STRANGE'S BROWNSTONE.
WHAT? WHAT'S THIS?
HOW DID YOU EVEN COME TO THIS DOOR?
UPPS
AVENGERS MANSION.
OH! I MUST THANK YOU VERY MUCH!
PATSY WALKER'S APARTMENT.
FINALLY, SHE PUT DOWN THAT SHAMPOO AD.
OH, THANK YOU!
WHADDYA GET, PATSY?
IT'S L'ENCHANTRESSE SHAMPOO.
I MUST TRY SOME RIGHT NOW.

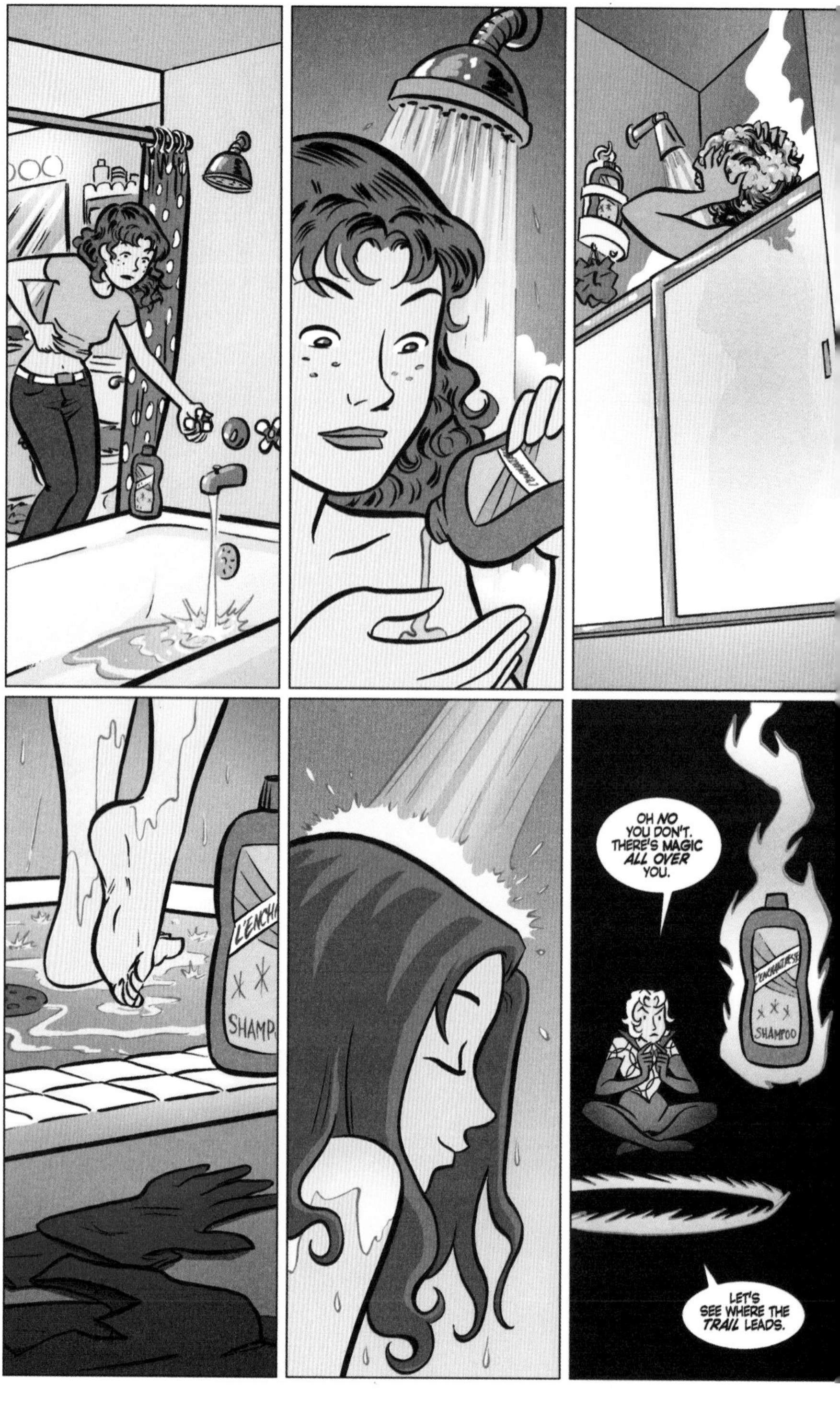
L'ENCHA
SHAMP
SHAMPOO
OH NO YOU DON'T. THERE'S MAGIC ALL OVER YOU.
LET'S SEE WHERE THE TRAIL LEADS.

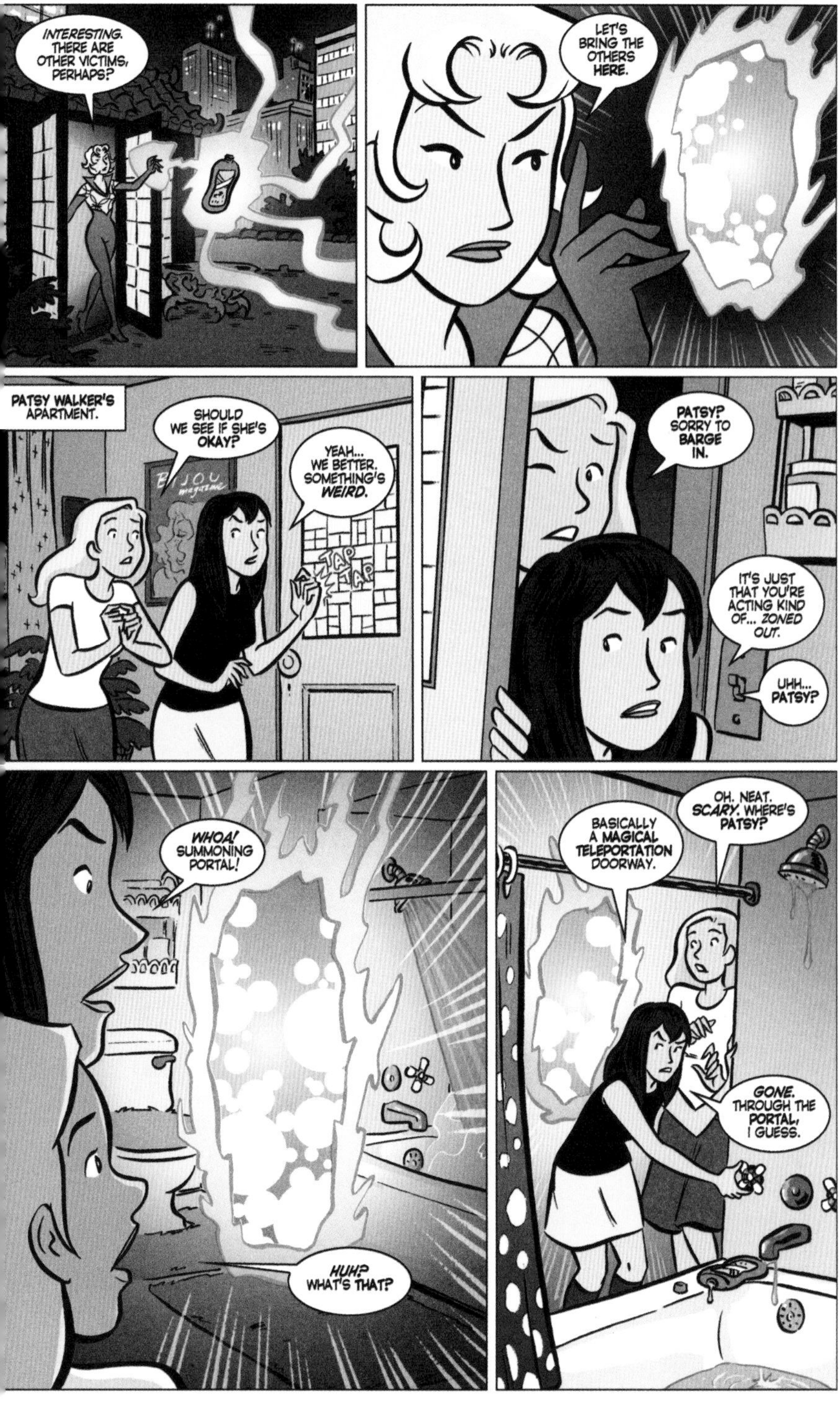
INTERESTING. THERE ARE OTHER VICTIMS, PERHAPS?
LET'S BRING THE OTHERS HERE.
PATSY WALKER'S APARTMENT.
SHOULD WE SEE IF SHE'S OKAY?
YEAH... WE BETTER. SOMETHING'S WEIRD.
TAP TAP
PATSY? SORRY TO BARGE IN.
IT'S JUST THAT YOU'RE ACTING KIND OF... ZONED OUT.
UHH... PATSY?
WHOA! SUMMONING PORTAL!
HUH? WHAT'S THAT?
BASICALLY A MAGICAL TELEPORTATION DOORWAY.
OH. NEAT. SCARY. WHERE'S PATSY?
GONE. THROUGH THE PORTAL, I GUESS.

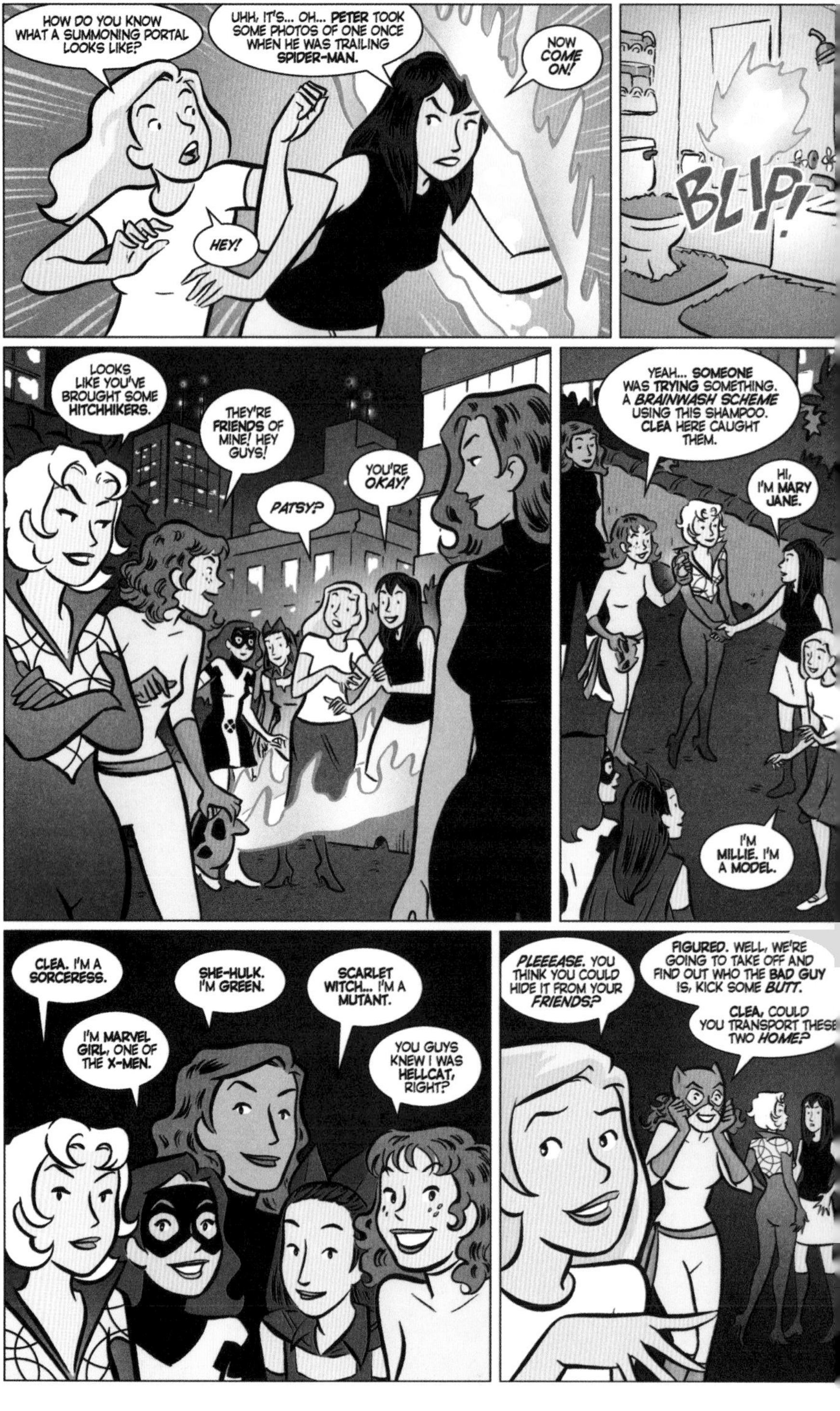
HOW DO YOU KNOW WHAT A SUMMONING PORTAL LOOKS LIKE?
UHH, IT'S... OH... PETER TOOK SOME PHOTOS OF ONE ONCE WHEN HE WAS TRAILING SPIDER-MAN.
NOW COME ON!
HEY!
BLIP!
LOOKS LIKE YOU'VE BROUGHT SOME HITCHHIKERS.
THEY'RE FRIENDS OF MINE! HEY GUYS!
PATSY?
YOU'RE OKAY!
YEAH... SOMEONE WAS TRYING SOMETHING. A BRAINWASH SCHEME USING THIS SHAMPOO. CLEA HERE CAUGHT THEM.
HI, I'M MARY JANE.
I'M MILLIE. I'M A MODEL.
CLEA. I'M A SORCERESS.
I'M MARVEL GIRL, ONE OF THE X-MEN.
SHE-HULK. I'M GREEN.
SCARLET WITCH... I'M A MUTANT.
YOU GUYS KNEW I WAS HELLCAT, RIGHT?
PLEEEASE. YOU THINK YOU COULD HIDE IT FROM YOUR FRIENDS?
FIGURED. WELL, WE'RE GOING TO TAKE OFF AND FIND OUT WHO THE BAD GUY IS, KICK SOME BUTT.
CLEA, COULD YOU TRANSPORT THESE TWO HOME?

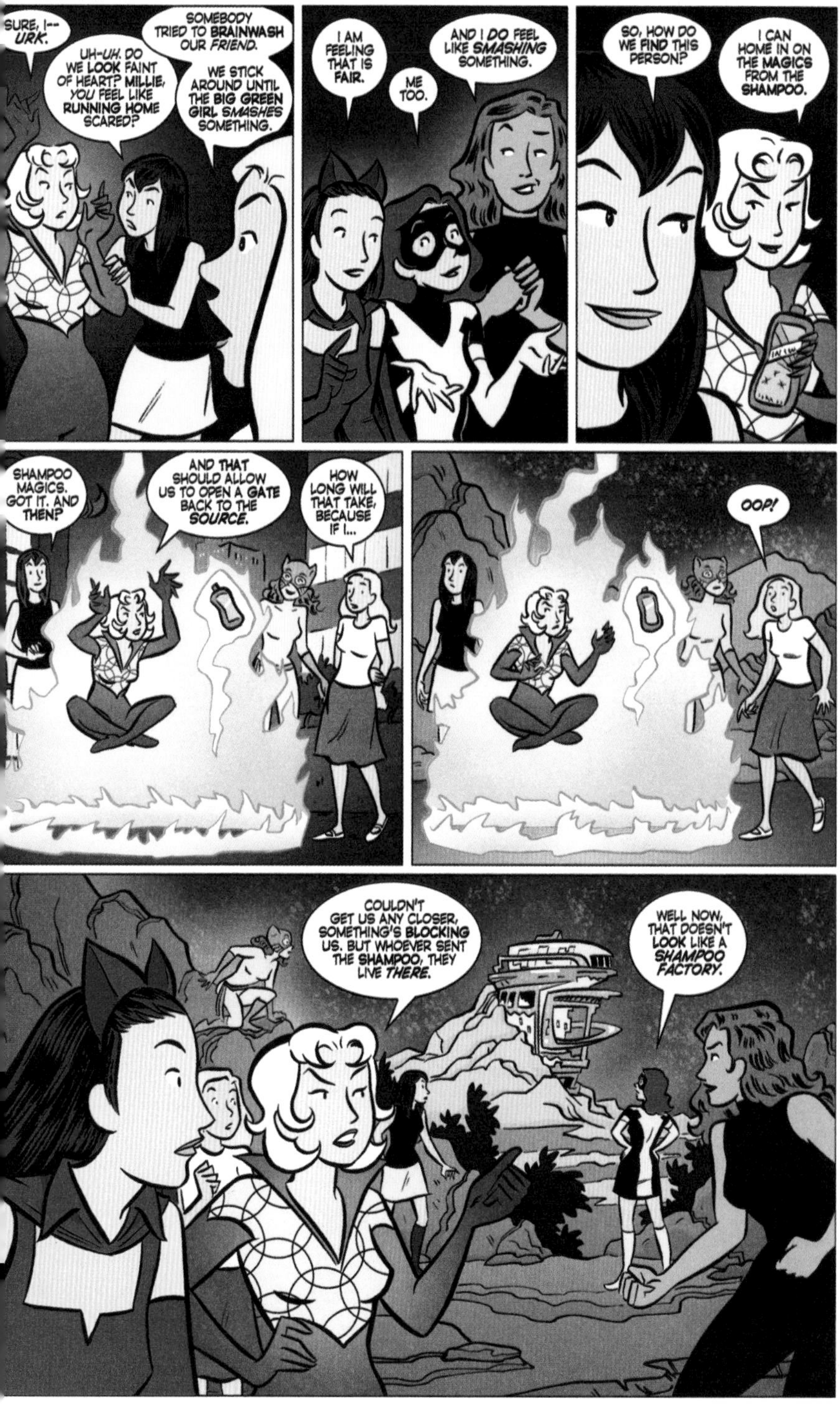

SURE, I-- URK.
UH-UH. DO WE LOOK FAINT OF HEART? MILLIE, YOU FEEL LIKE RUNNING HOME SCARED?
SOMEBODY TRIED TO BRAINWASH OUR FRIEND.
WE STICK AROUND UNTIL THE BIG GREEN GIRL SMASHES SOMETHING.
I AM FEELING THAT IS FAIR.
ME TOO.
AND I DO FEEL LIKE SMASHING SOMETHING.
SO, HOW DO WE FIND THIS PERSON?
I CAN HOME IN ON THE MAGICS FROM THE SHAMPOO.
SHAMPOO MAGICS. GOT IT. AND THEN?
AND THAT SHOULD ALLOW US TO OPEN A GATE BACK TO THE SOURCE.
HOW LONG WILL THAT TAKE, BECAUSE IF I...
OOP!
COULDN'T GET US ANY CLOSER. SOMETHING'S BLOCKING US. BUT WHOEVER SENT THE SHAMPOO, THEY LIVE THERE.
WELL NOW, THAT DOESN'T LOOK LIKE A SHAMPOO FACTORY.

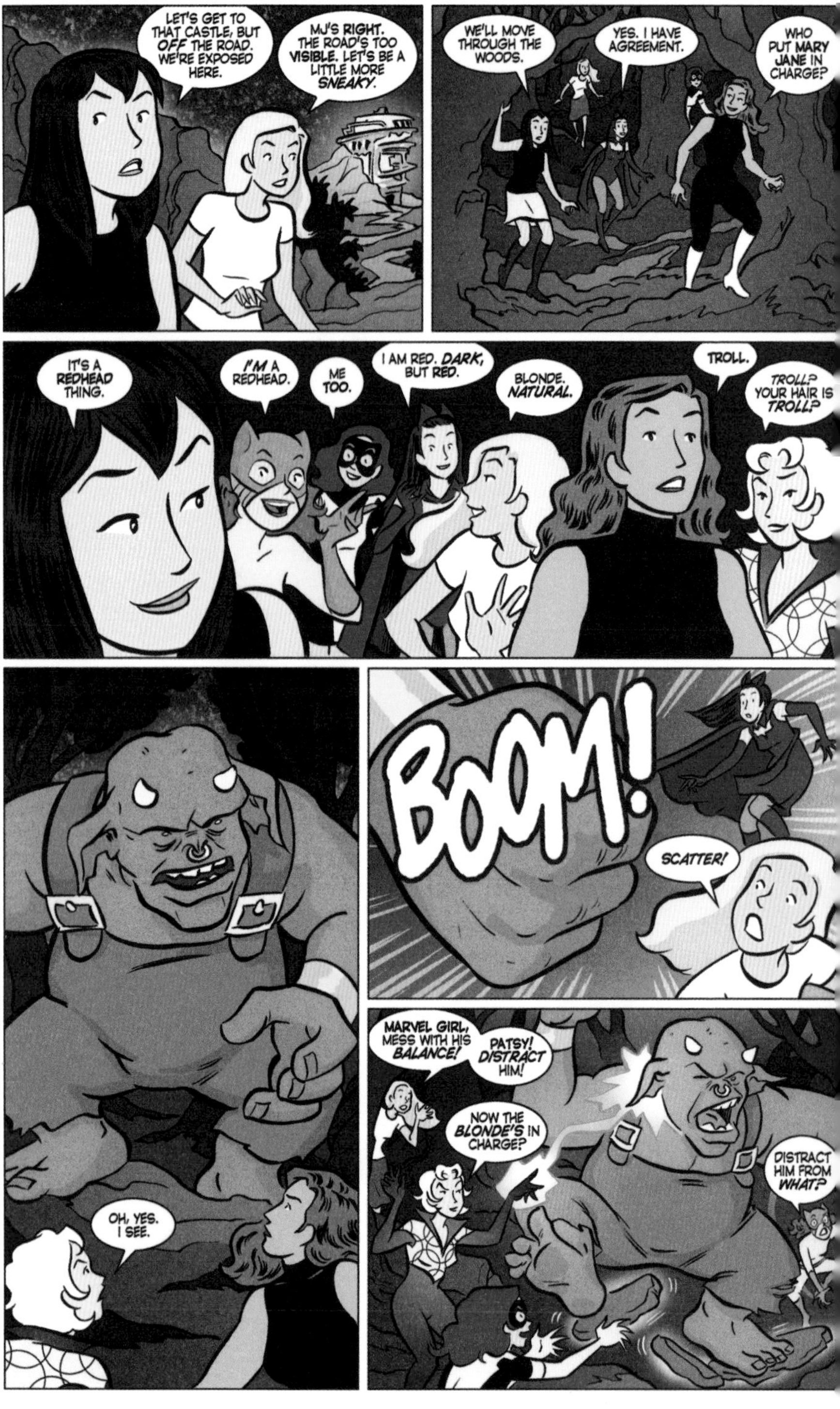
LET'S GET TO THAT CASTLE, BUT OFF THE ROAD. WE'RE EXPOSED HERE.
MJ'S RIGHT. THE ROAD'S TOO VISIBLE. LET'S BE A LITTLE MORE SNEAKY.
WE'LL MOVE THROUGH THE WOODS.
YES. I HAVE AGREEMENT.
WHO PUT MARY JANE IN CHARGE?
IT'S A REDHEAD THING.
I'M A REDHEAD.
ME TOO.
I AM RED. DARK, BUT RED.
BLONDE. NATURAL.
TROLL.
TROLL? YOUR HAIR IS TROLL?
OH, YES. I SEE.
BOOM!
SCATTER!
MARVEL GIRL, MESS WITH HIS BALANCE!
PATSY! DISTRACT HIM!
NOW THE BLONDE'S IN CHARGE?
DISTRACT HIM FROM WHAT?

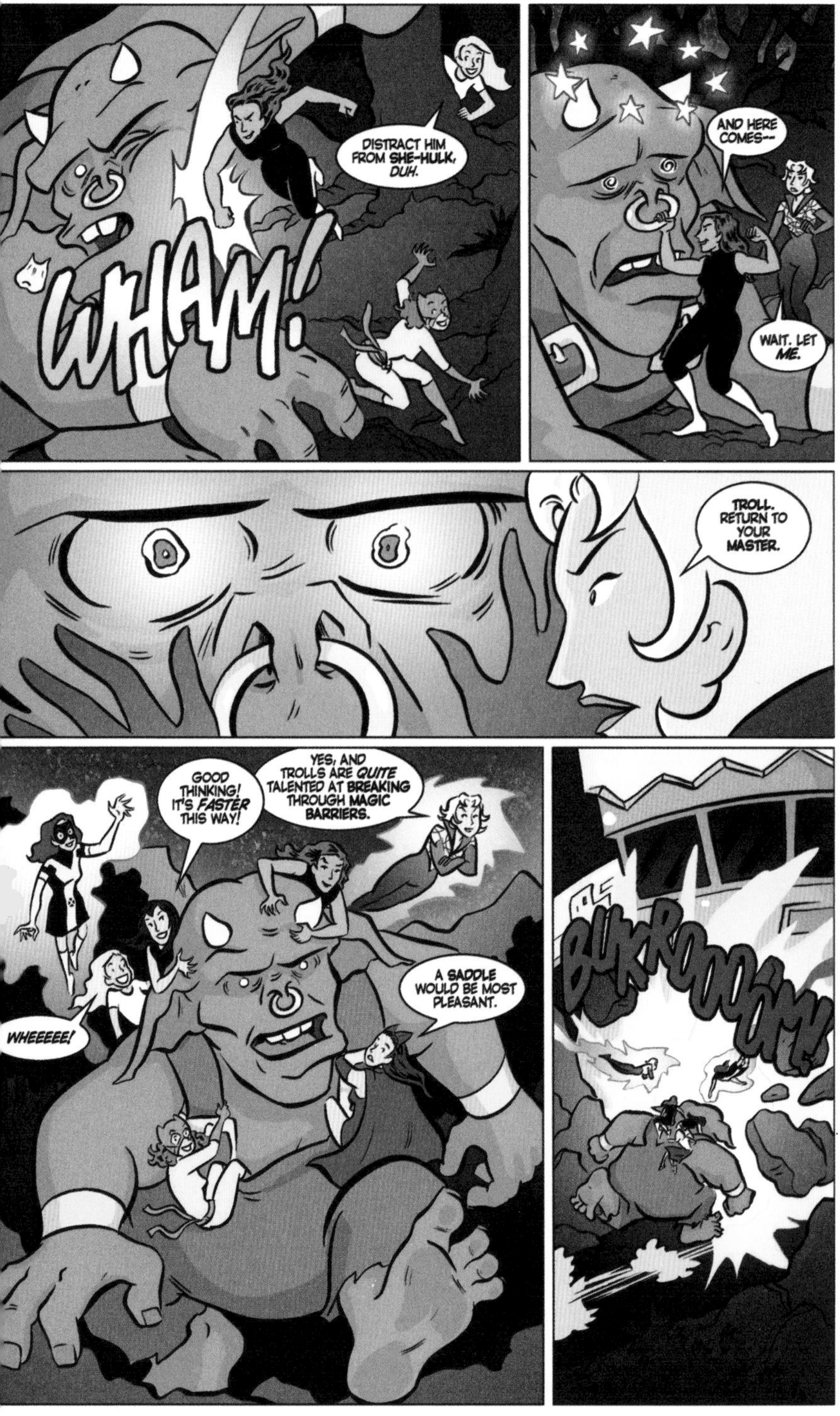
DISTRACT HIM FROM SHE-HULK, DUH.
WHAM!
AND HERE COMES--
WAIT. LET ME.
TROLL. RETURN TO YOUR MASTER.
GOOD THINKING! IT'S FASTER THIS WAY!
YES, AND TROLLS ARE QUITE TALENTED AT BREAKING THROUGH MAGIC BARRIERS.
WHEEEEE!
A SADDLE WOULD BE MOST PLEASANT.
BUKROOOOOM!

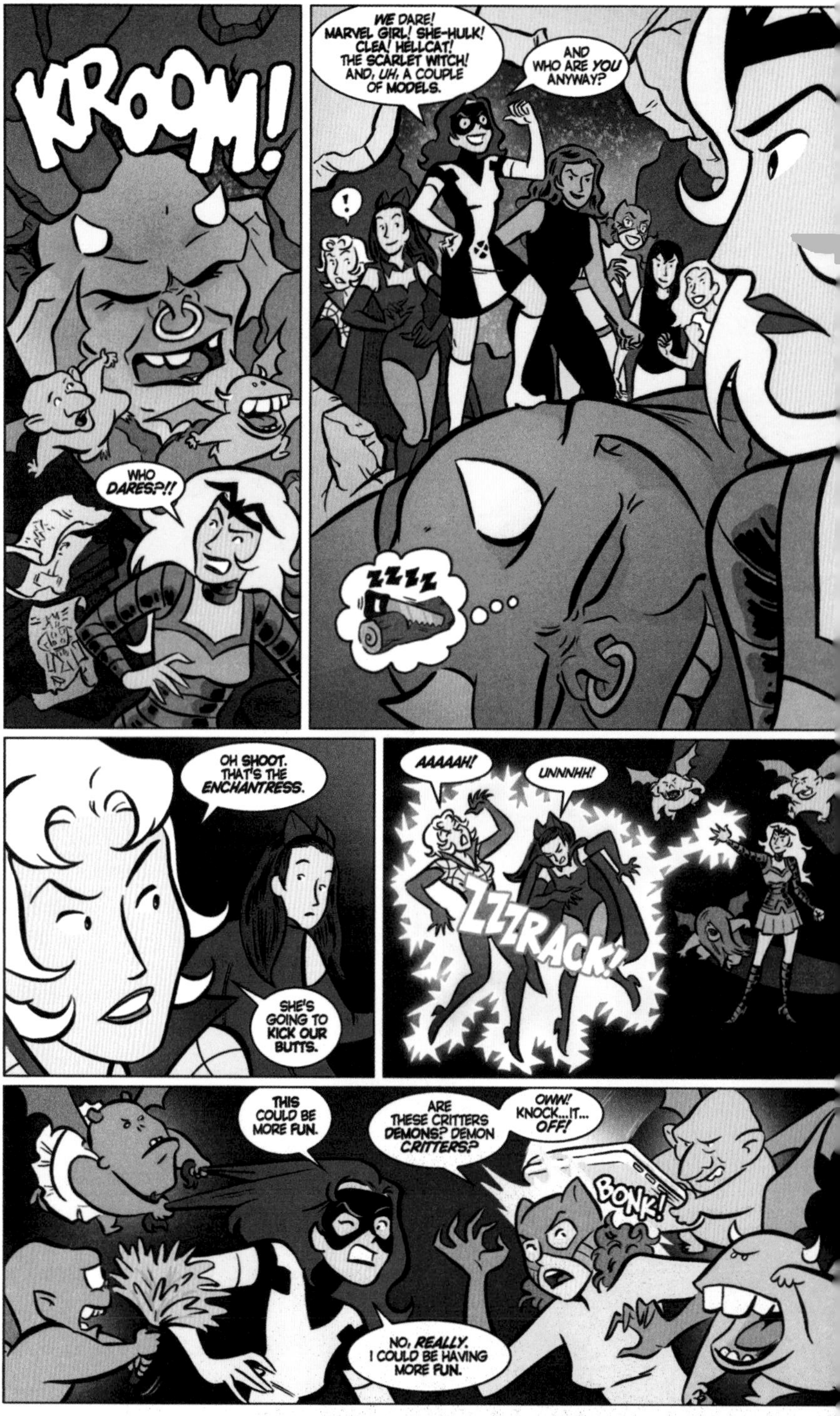
KROOM!
WHO DARES?!!
WE DARE! MARVEL GIRL! SHE-HULK! CLEA! HELLCAT! THE SCARLET WITCH! AND, UH, A COUPLE OF MODELS.
AND WHO ARE YOU ANYWAY?
!
ZZZZ
OH SHOOT. THAT'S THE ENCHANTRESS.
SHE'S GOING TO KICK OUR BUTTS.
AAAAAH!
UNNNHH!
ZZZRACK!
THIS COULD BE MORE FUN.
ARE THESE CRITTERS DEMONS? DEMON CRITTERS?
OWW! KNOCK...IT... OFF!
BONK!
NO, REALLY. I COULD BE HAVING MORE FUN.

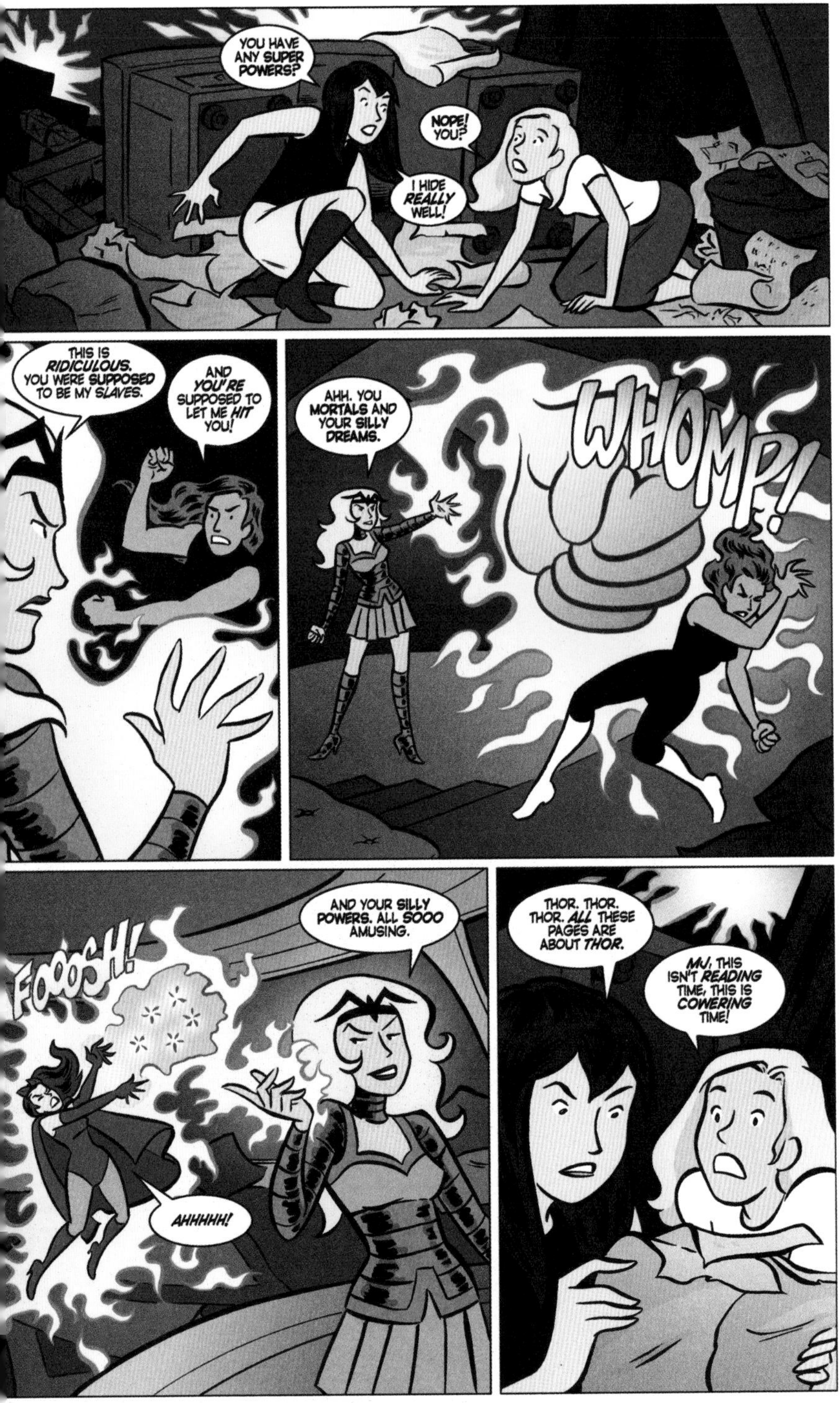

YOU HAVE ANY SUPER POWERS?
NOPE! YOU?
I HIDE REALLY WELL!
THIS IS RIDICULOUS. YOU WERE SUPPOSED TO BE MY SLAVES.
AND YOU'RE SUPPOSED TO LET ME HIT YOU!
AHH. YOU MORTALS AND YOUR SILLY DREAMS.
WHOMP!
AND YOUR SILLY POWERS. ALL SOOO AMUSING.
FOOOSH!
AHHHHH!
THOR. THOR. THOR. ALL THESE PAGES ARE ABOUT THOR.
MJ, THIS ISN'T READING TIME, THIS IS COWERING TIME!

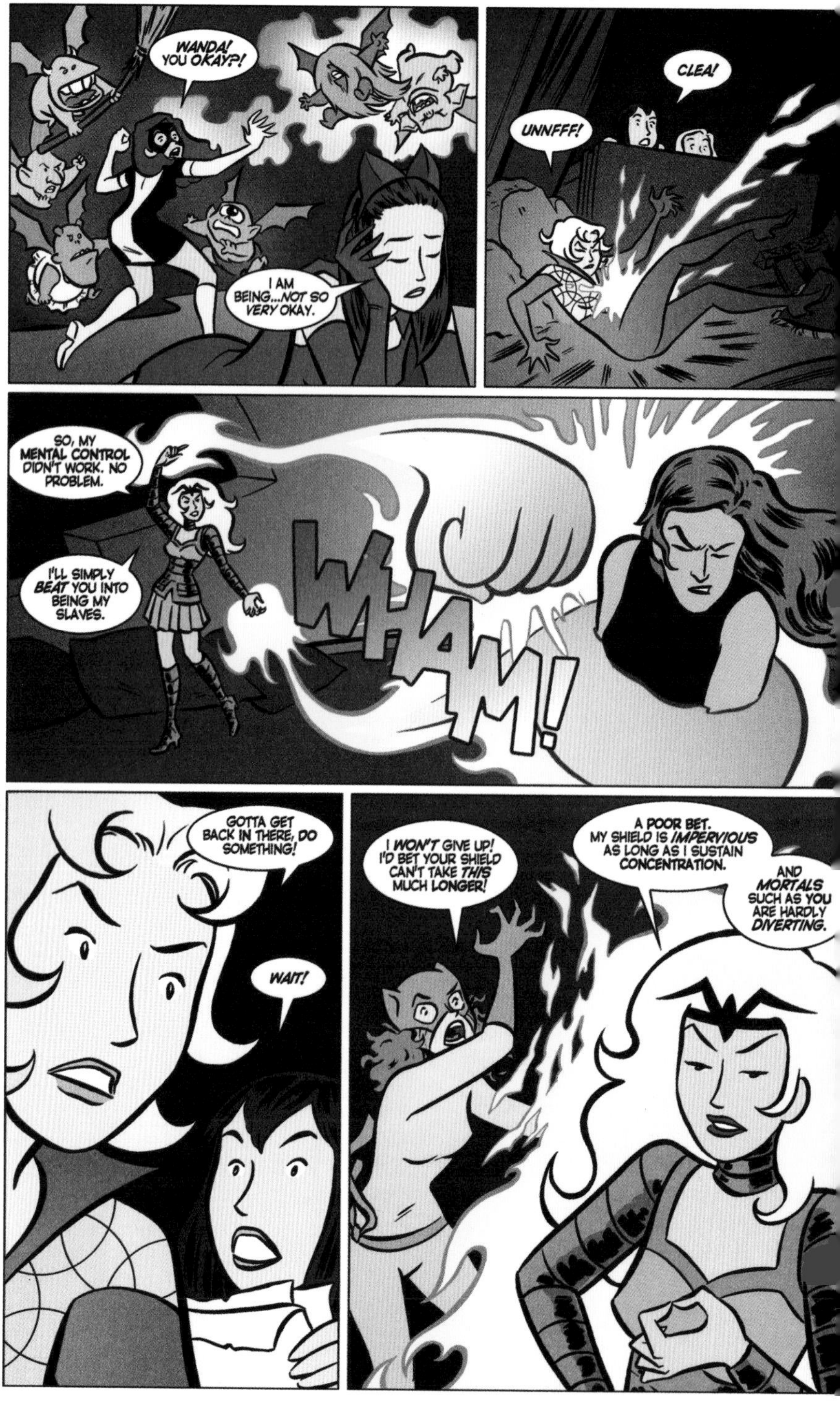
WANDA! YOU OKAY?!
I AM BEING...NOT SO VERY OKAY.
CLEA!
UNNFFF!
SO, MY MENTAL CONTROL DIDN'T WORK. NO PROBLEM.
I'LL SIMPLY BEAT YOU INTO BEING MY SLAVES.
WHAM!
GOTTA GET BACK IN THERE, DO SOMETHING!
WAIT!
I WON'T GIVE UP! I'D BET YOUR SHIELD CAN'T TAKE THIS MUCH LONGER!
A POOR BET. MY SHIELD IS IMPERVIOUS AS LONG AS I SUSTAIN CONCENTRATION.
AND MORTALS SUCH AS YOU ARE HARDLY DIVERTING.

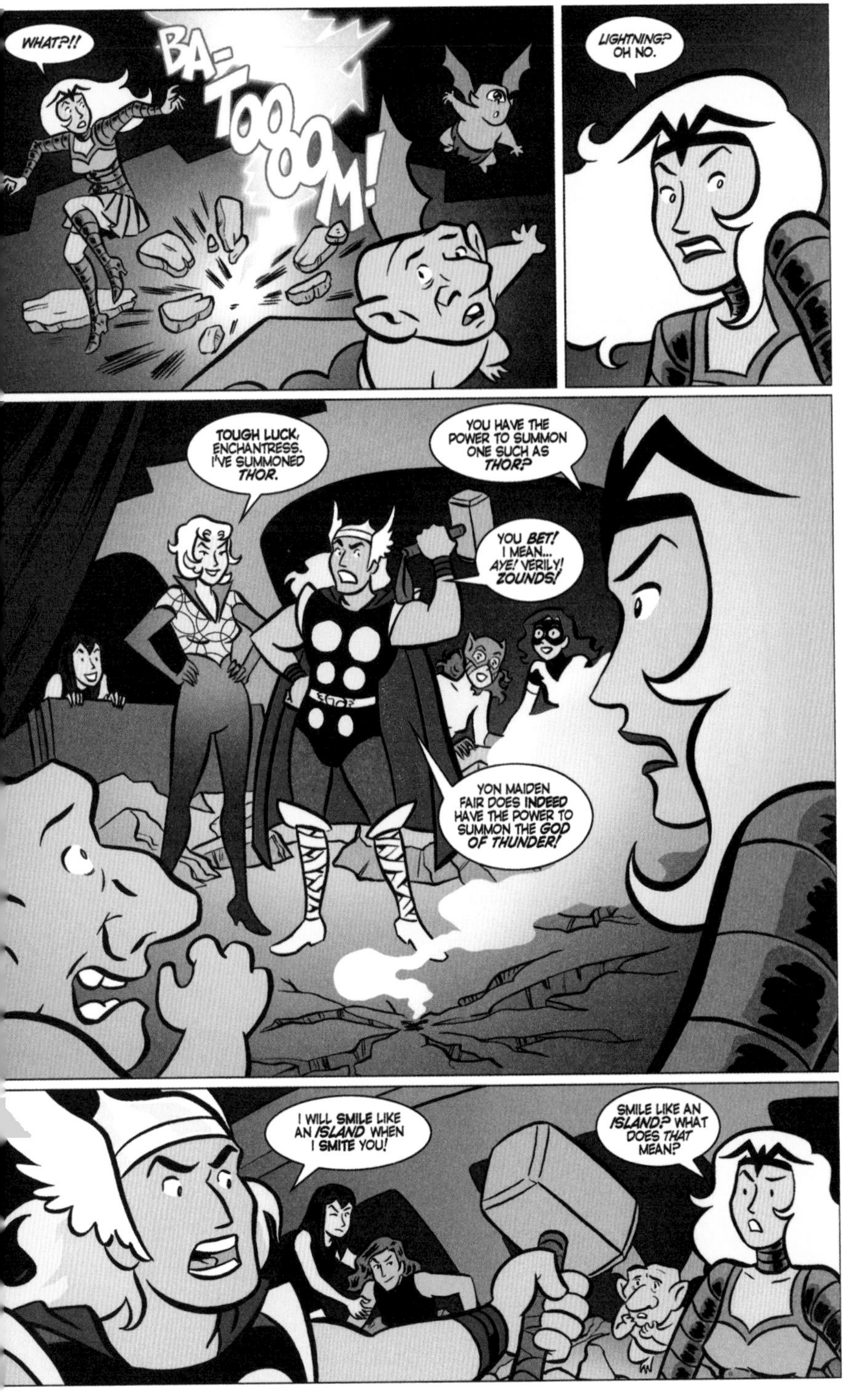
WHAT?!!
BA-TOOOOM!
LIGHTNING? OH NO.
TOUGH LUCK, ENCHANTRESS. I'VE SUMMONED THOR.
YOU HAVE THE POWER TO SUMMON ONE SUCH AS THOR?
YOU BET! I MEAN... AYE! VERILY! ZOUNDS!
YON MAIDEN FAIR DOES INDEED HAVE THE POWER TO SUMMON THE GOD OF THUNDER!
I WILL SMILE LIKE AN ISLAND WHEN I SMITE YOU!
SMILE LIKE AN ISLAND? WHAT DOES THAT MEAN?

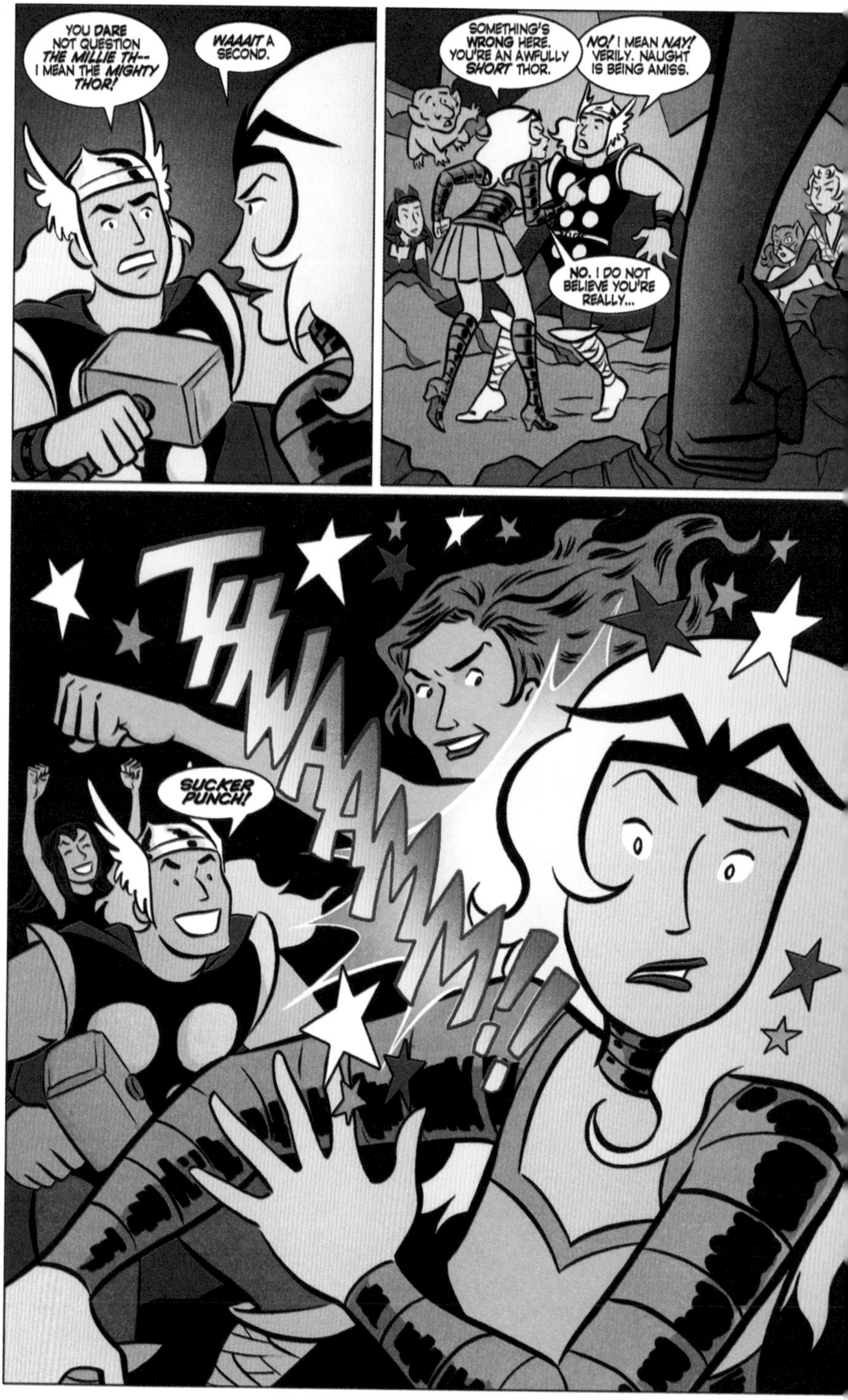

YOU DARE NOT QUESTION THE MILLIE TH-- I MEAN THE MIGHTY THOR!
WAAAIT A SECOND.
SOMETHING'S WRONG HERE. YOU'RE AN AWFULLY SHORT THOR.
NO! I MEAN NAY! VERILY. NAUGHT IS BEING AMISS.
NO. I DO NOT BELIEVE YOU'RE REALLY...
THWAAMMM!!!
SUCKER PUNCH!

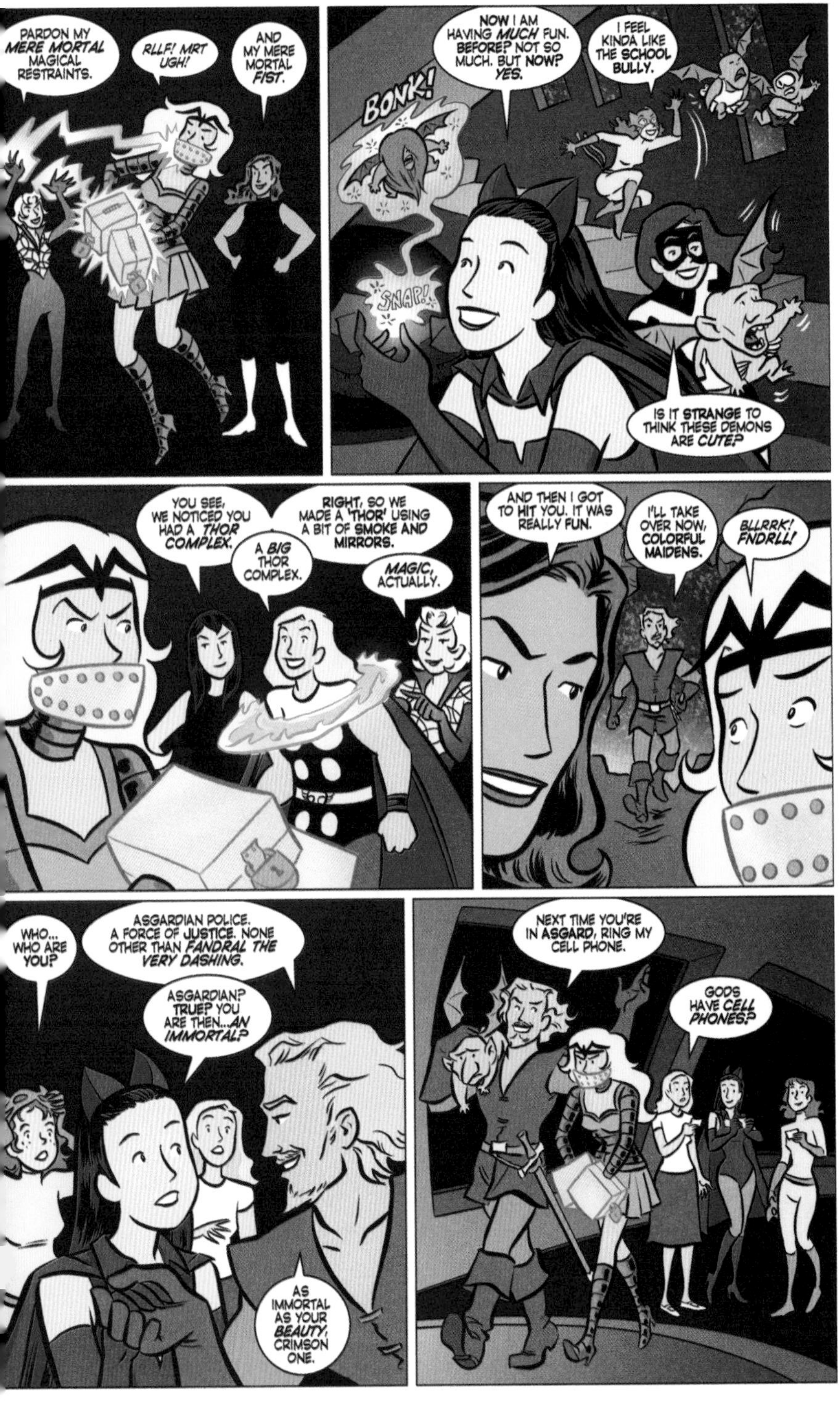
PARDON MY MERE MORTAL MAGICAL RESTRAINTS.
RLLF! MRT UGH!
AND MY MERE MORTAL FIST.
NOW I AM HAVING MUCH FUN. BEFORE? NOT SO MUCH. BUT NOW? YES.
I FEEL KINDA LIKE THE SCHOOL BULLY.
BONK!
SNAP!
IS IT STRANGE TO THINK THESE DEMONS ARE CUTE?
YOU SEE, WE NOTICED YOU HAD A THOR COMPLEX.
A BIG THOR COMPLEX.
RIGHT, SO WE MADE A 'THOR' USING A BIT OF SMOKE AND MIRRORS.
MAGIC, ACTUALLY.
AND THEN I GOT TO HIT YOU. IT WAS REALLY FUN.
I'LL TAKE OVER NOW, COLORFUL MAIDENS.
BLLRRK! FNDRLL!
WHO... WHO ARE YOU?
ASGARDIAN POLICE. A FORCE OF JUSTICE. NONE OTHER THAN FANDRAL THE VERY DASHING.
ASGARDIAN? TRUE? YOU ARE THEN...AN IMMORTAL?
AS IMMORTAL AS YOUR BEAUTY, CRIMSON ONE.
NEXT TIME YOU'RE IN ASGARD, RING MY CELL PHONE.
GODS HAVE CELL PHONES?

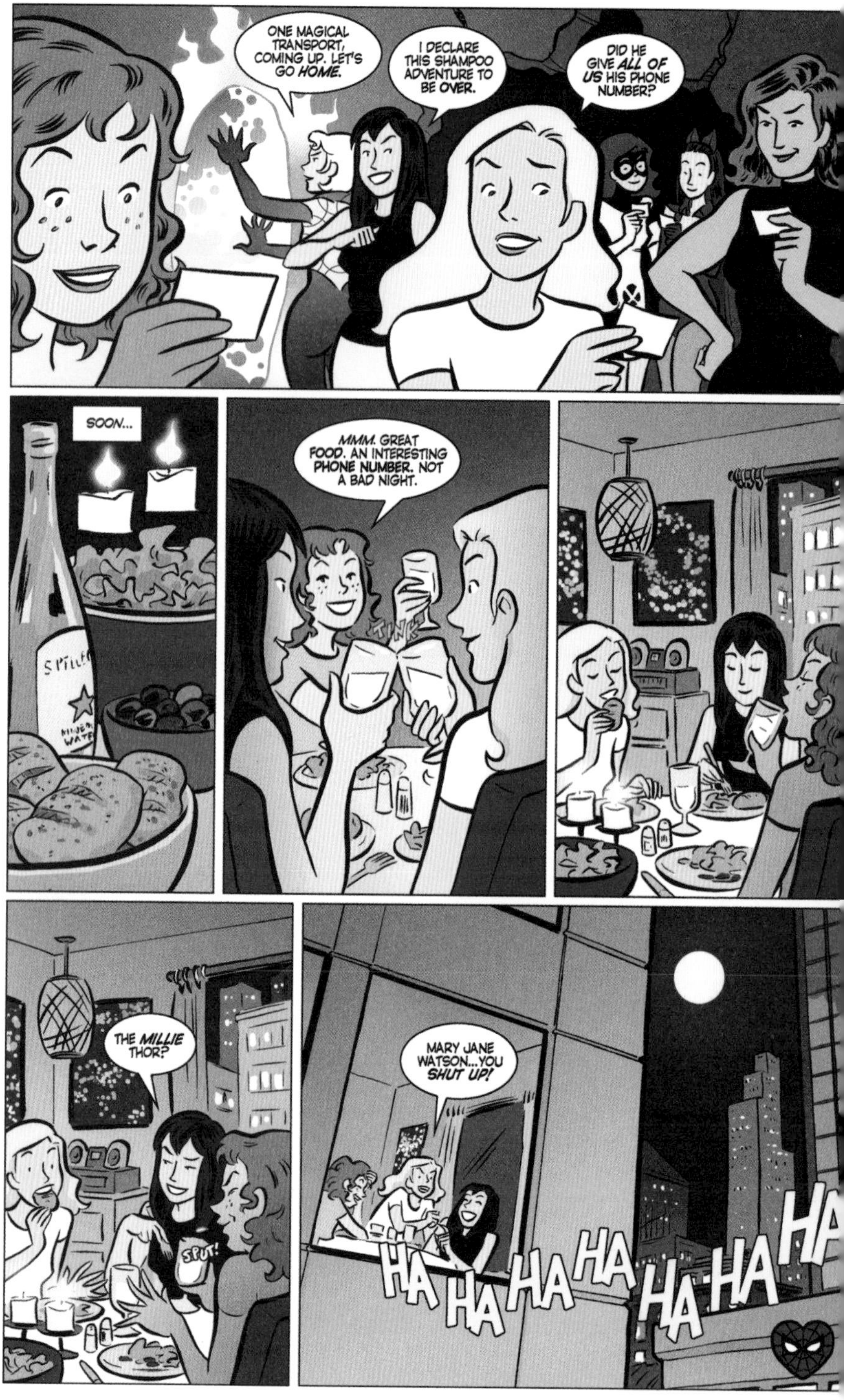
ONE MAGICAL TRANSPORT, COMING UP. LET'S GO *HOME*.
I DECLARE THIS SHAMPOO ADVENTURE TO BE *OVER*.
DID HE GIVE *ALL OF US* HIS PHONE NUMBER?
SOON...
MMM. GREAT FOOD. AN INTERESTING PHONE NUMBER. NOT A BAD NIGHT.
TINK
THE *MILLIE* THOR?
SPUT!
MARY JANE WATSON...YOU *SHUT UP!*
HA HA HA HA HA HA HA

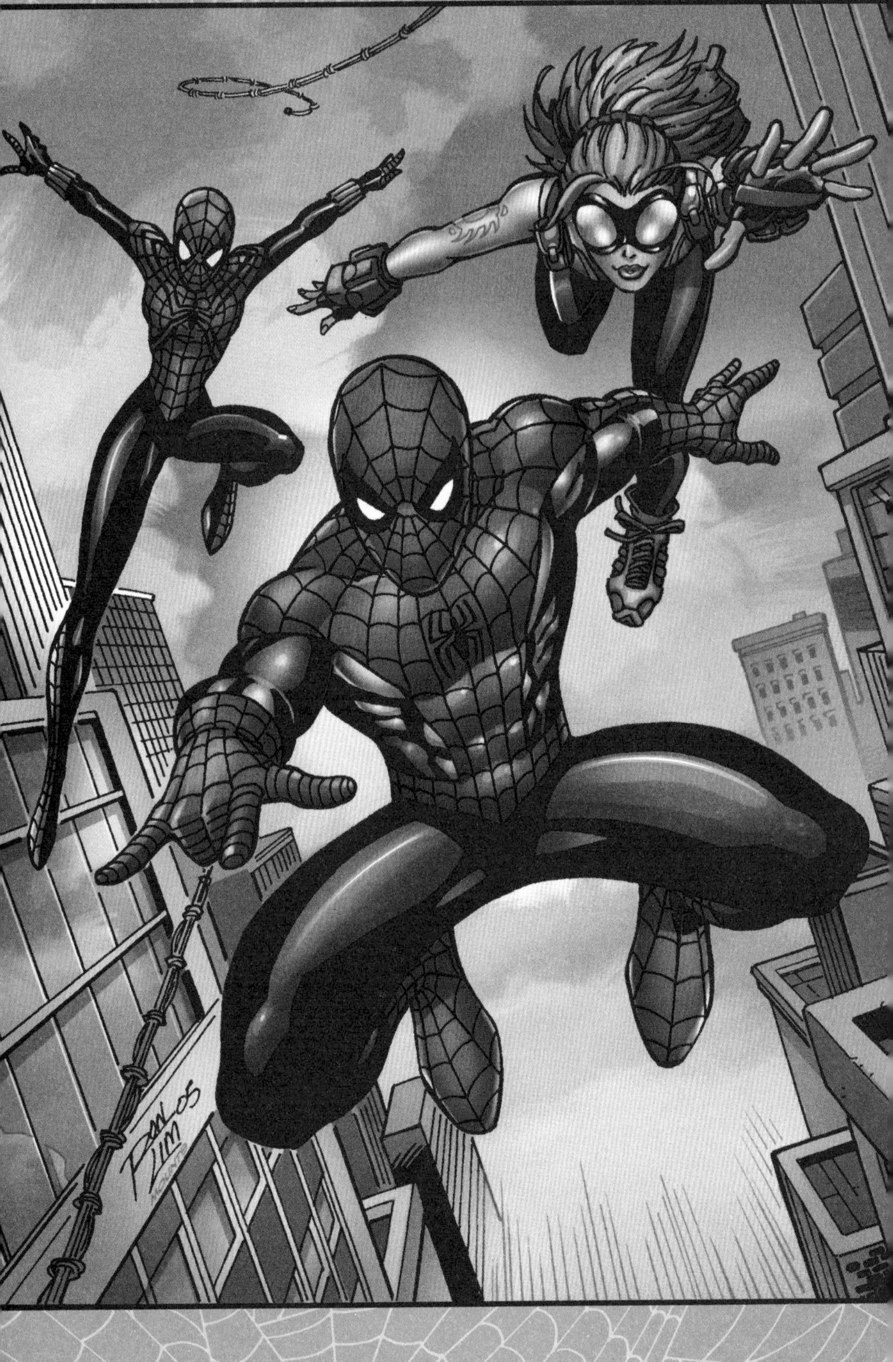

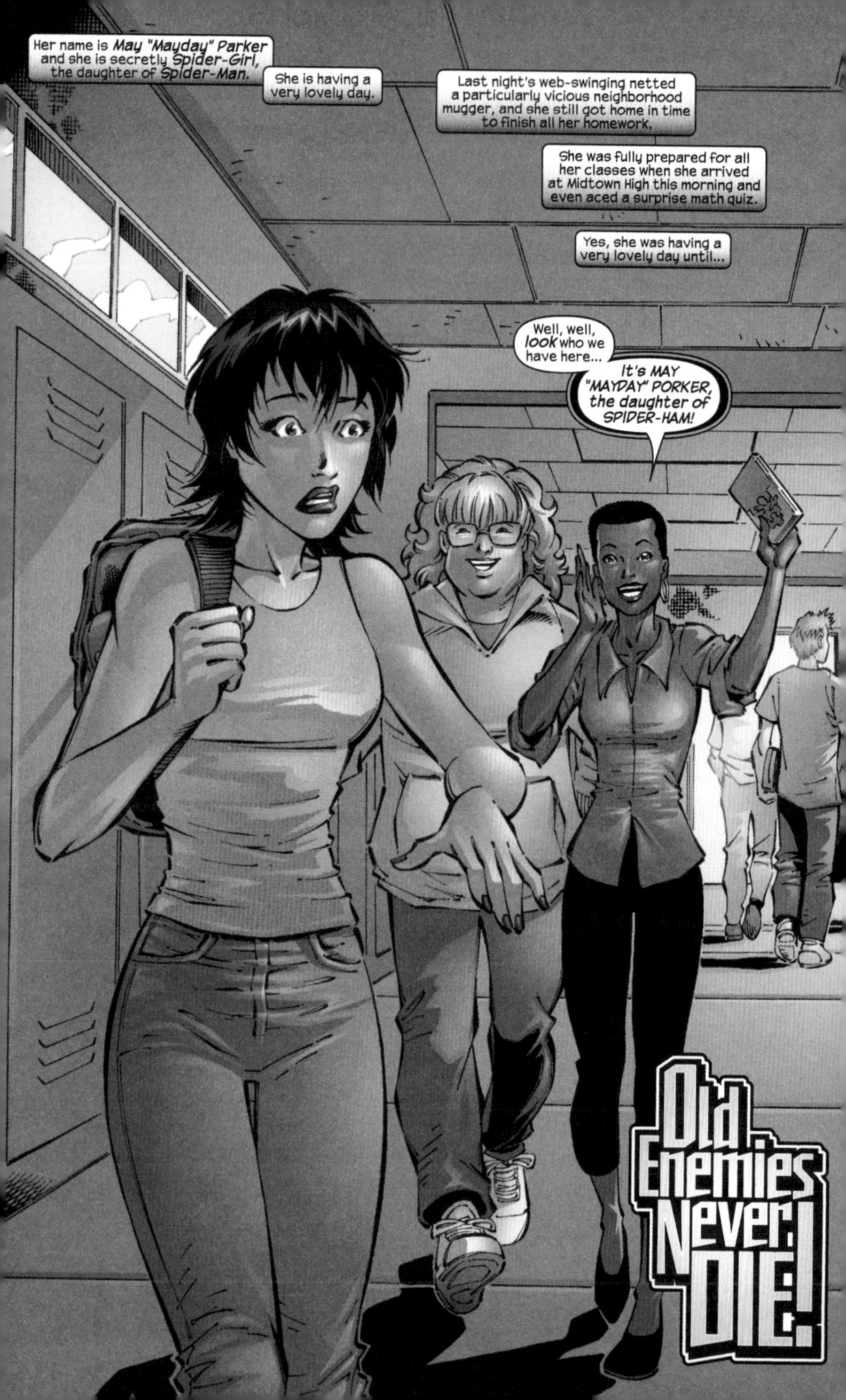
Her name is May "Mayday" Parker and she is secretly Spider-Girl, the daughter of Spider-Man.
She is having a very lovely day.
Last night's web-swinging netted a particularly vicious neighborhood mugger, and she still got home in time to finish all her homework.
She was fully prepared for all her classes when she arrived at Midtown High this morning and even aced a surprise math quiz.
Yes, she was having a very lovely day until...
Well, well, look who we have here...
It's MAY "MAYDAY" PORKER, the daughter of SPIDER-HAM!
Old Enemies Never Die!

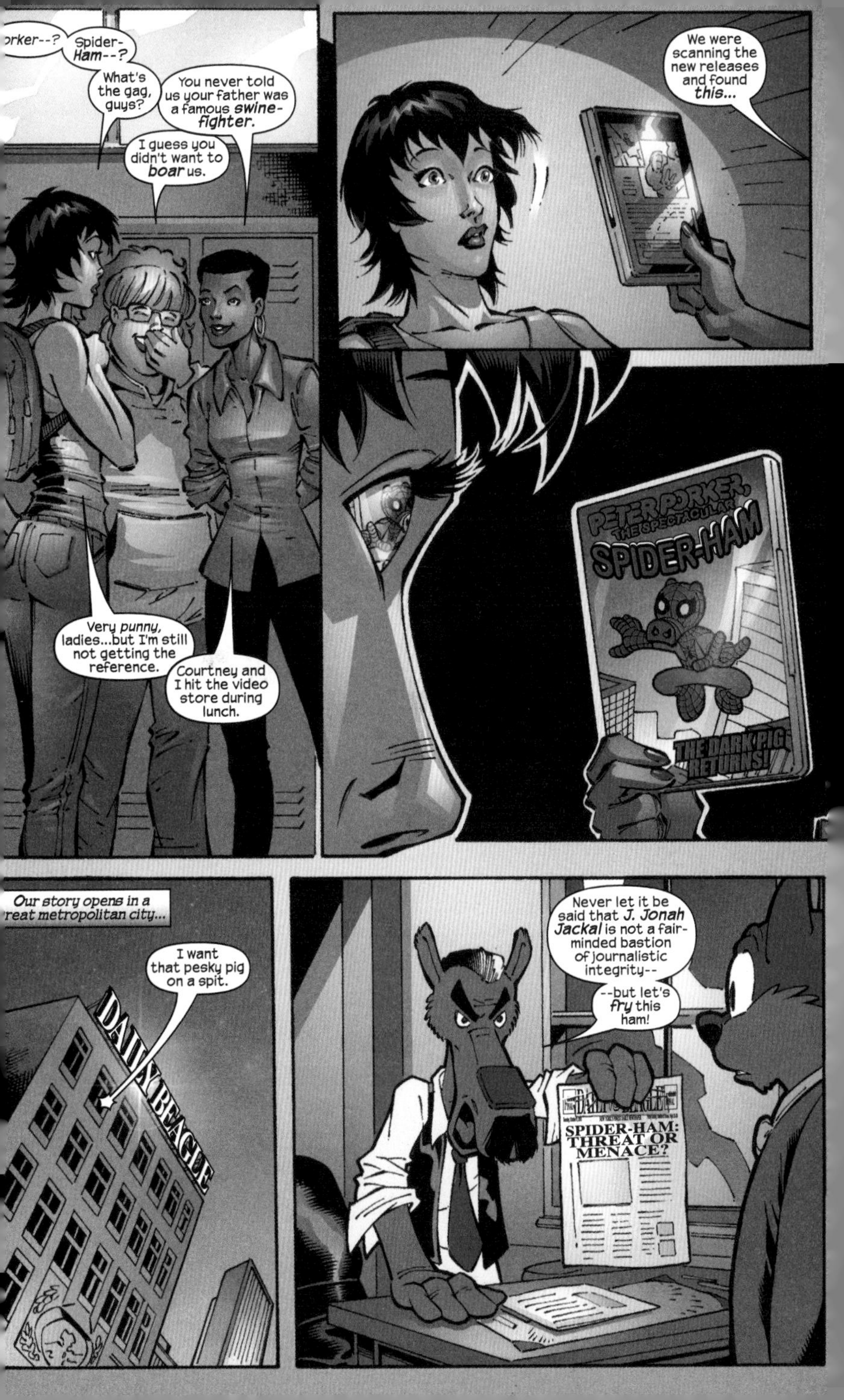

orker--?
Spider-Ham--?
What's the gag, guys?
You never told us your father was a famous *swine-fighter*.
I guess you didn't want to *boar* us.
We were scanning the new releases and found *this*...
Very *punny*, ladies...but I'm still not getting the reference.
Courtney and I hit the video store during lunch.
PETER PORKER, THE SPECTACULAR SPIDER-HAM
THE DARK PIG RETURNS!
Our story opens in a reat metropolitan city...
I want that pesky pig on a spit.
DAILY BEAGLE
Never let it be said that *J. Jonah Jackal* is not a fair-minded bastion of journalistic integrity--
--but let's *fry* this ham!
SPIDER-HAM: THREAT OR MENACE?

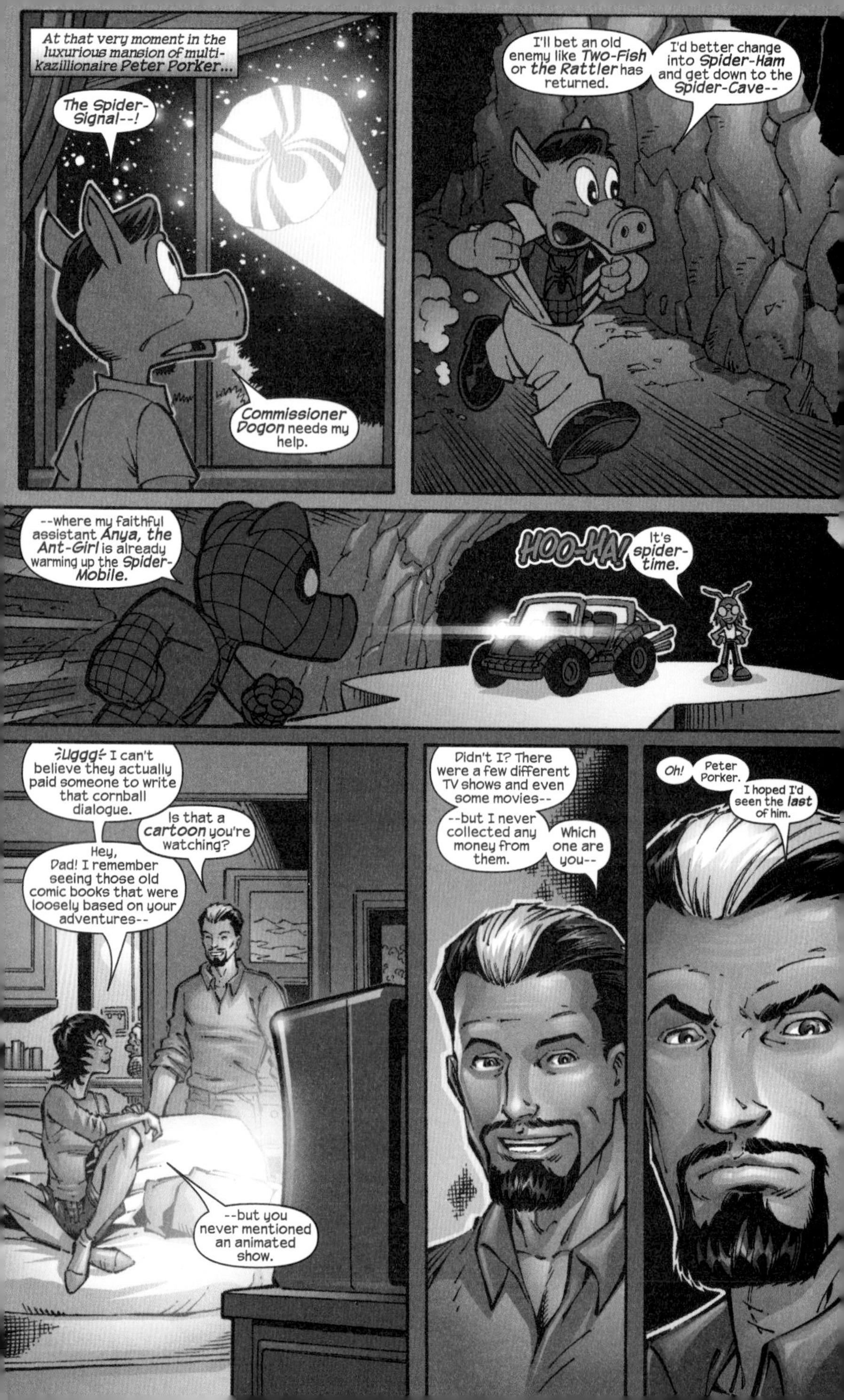
At that very moment in the luxurious mansion of multi-kazillionaire Peter Porker...
The Spider-Signal--!
Commissioner Dogon needs my help.
I'll bet an old enemy like Two-Fish or the Rattler has returned.
I'd better change into Spider-Ham and get down to the Spider-Cave--
--where my faithful assistant Anya, the Ant-Girl is already warming up the Spider-Mobile.
HOO-HA!
It's spider-time.
Uggg I can't believe they actually paid someone to write that cornball dialogue.
Is that a cartoon you're watching?
Hey, Dad! I remember seeing those old comic books that were loosely based on your adventures--
--but you never mentioned an animated show.
Didn't I? There were a few different TV shows and even some movies--
--but I never collected any money from them.
Which one are you--
Oh!
Peter Porker.
I hoped I'd seen the last of him.

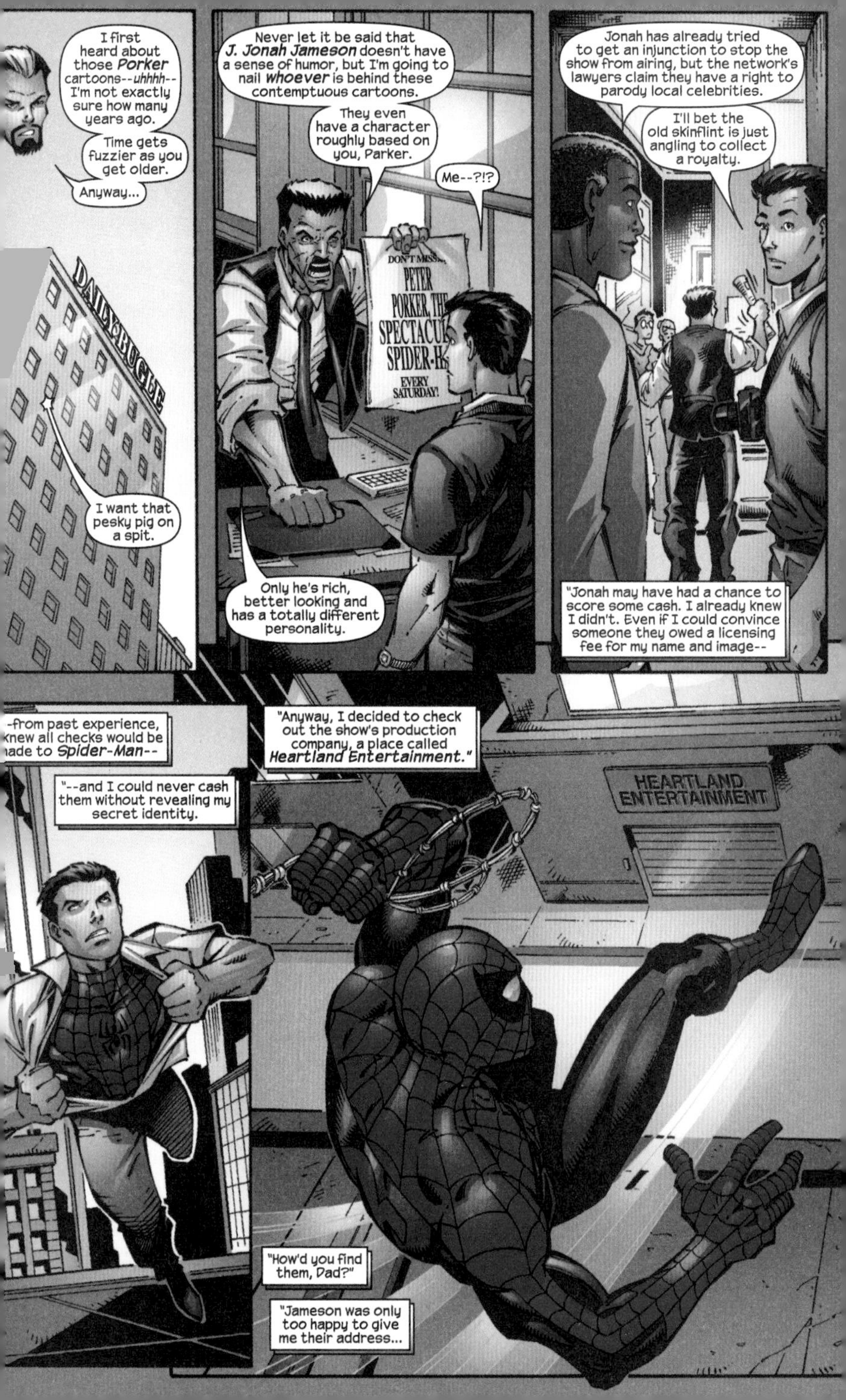

I first heard about those Porker cartoons--uhhhh--I'm not exactly sure how many years ago.
Time gets fuzzier as you get older.
Anyway...
I want that pesky pig on a spit.
Never let it be said that J. Jonah Jameson doesn't have a sense of humor, but I'm going to nail whoever is behind these contemptuous cartoons.
They even have a character roughly based on you, Parker.
Me--?!?
DON'T MISS... PETER PORKER, THE SPECTACU... SPIDER-H... EVERY SATURDAY!
Only he's rich, better looking and has a totally different personality.
Jonah has already tried to get an injunction to stop the show from airing, but the network's lawyers claim they have a right to parody local celebrities.
I'll bet the old skinflint is just angling to collect a royalty.
"Jonah may have had a chance to score some cash. I already knew I didn't. Even if I could convince someone they owed a licensing fee for my name and image--
-from past experience, knew all checks would be made to Spider-Man--
"--and I could never cash them without revealing my secret identity.
"Anyway, I decided to check out the show's production company, a place called Heartland Entertainment."
HEARTLAND ENTERTAINMENT
"How'd you find them, Dad?"
"Jameson was only too happy to give me their address...

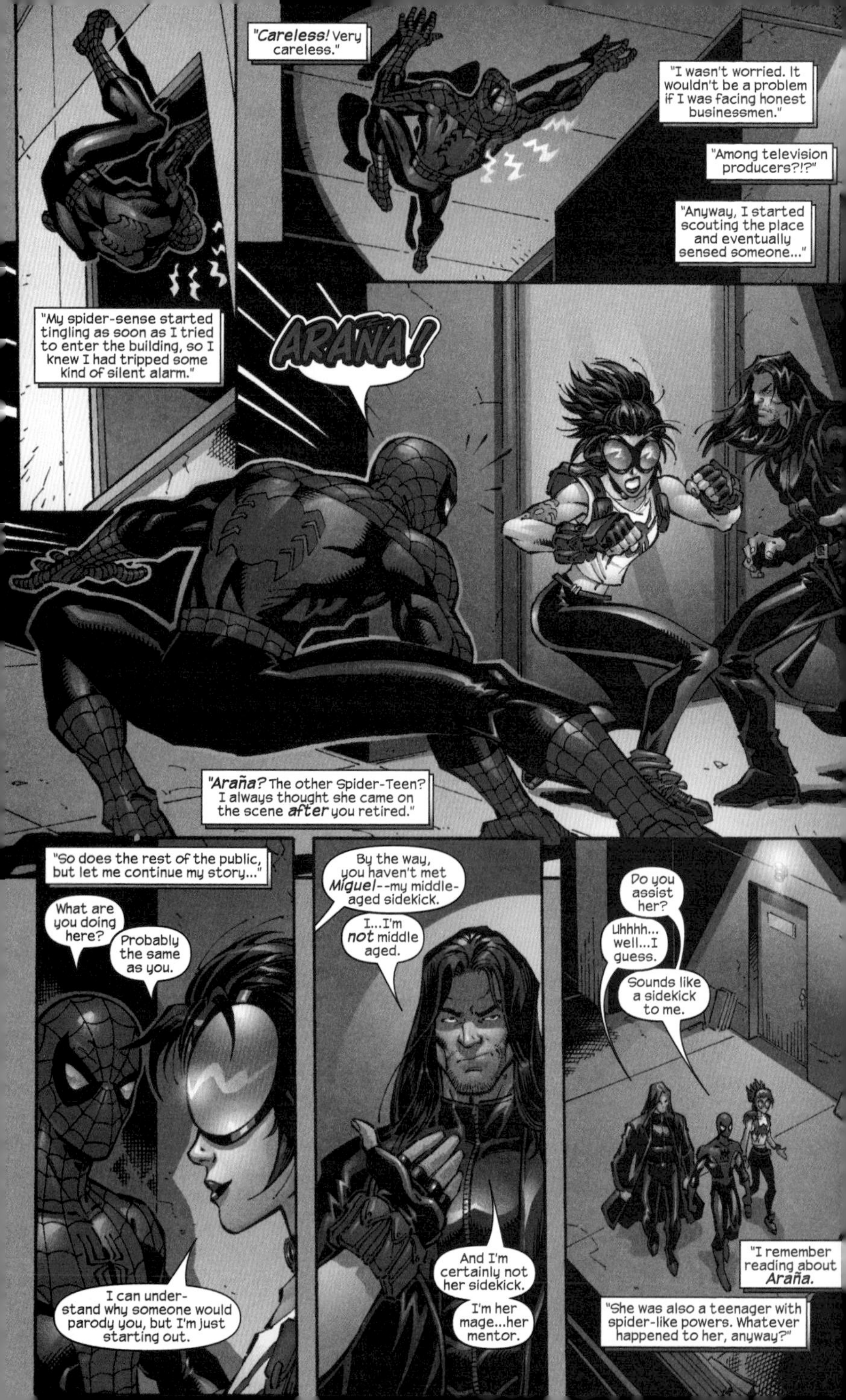
"Careless! Very careless."
"I wasn't worried. It wouldn't be a problem if I was facing honest businessmen."
"Among television producers?!?"
"Anyway, I started scouting the place and eventually sensed someone..."
"My spider-sense started tingling as soon as I tried to enter the building, so I knew I had tripped some kind of silent alarm."
ARAÑA!
"Araña? The other Spider-Teen? I always thought she came on the scene after you retired."
"So does the rest of the public, but let me continue my story..."
What are you doing here?
Probably the same as you.
I can under-stand why someone would parody you, but I'm just starting out.
By the way, you haven't met Miguel--my middle-aged sidekick.
I...I'm not middle aged.
And I'm certainly not her sidekick.
I'm her mage...her mentor.
Do you assist her?
Uhhhh... well...I guess.
Sounds like a sidekick to me.
"I remember reading about Araña.
"She was also a teenager with spider-like powers. Whatever happened to her, anyway?"

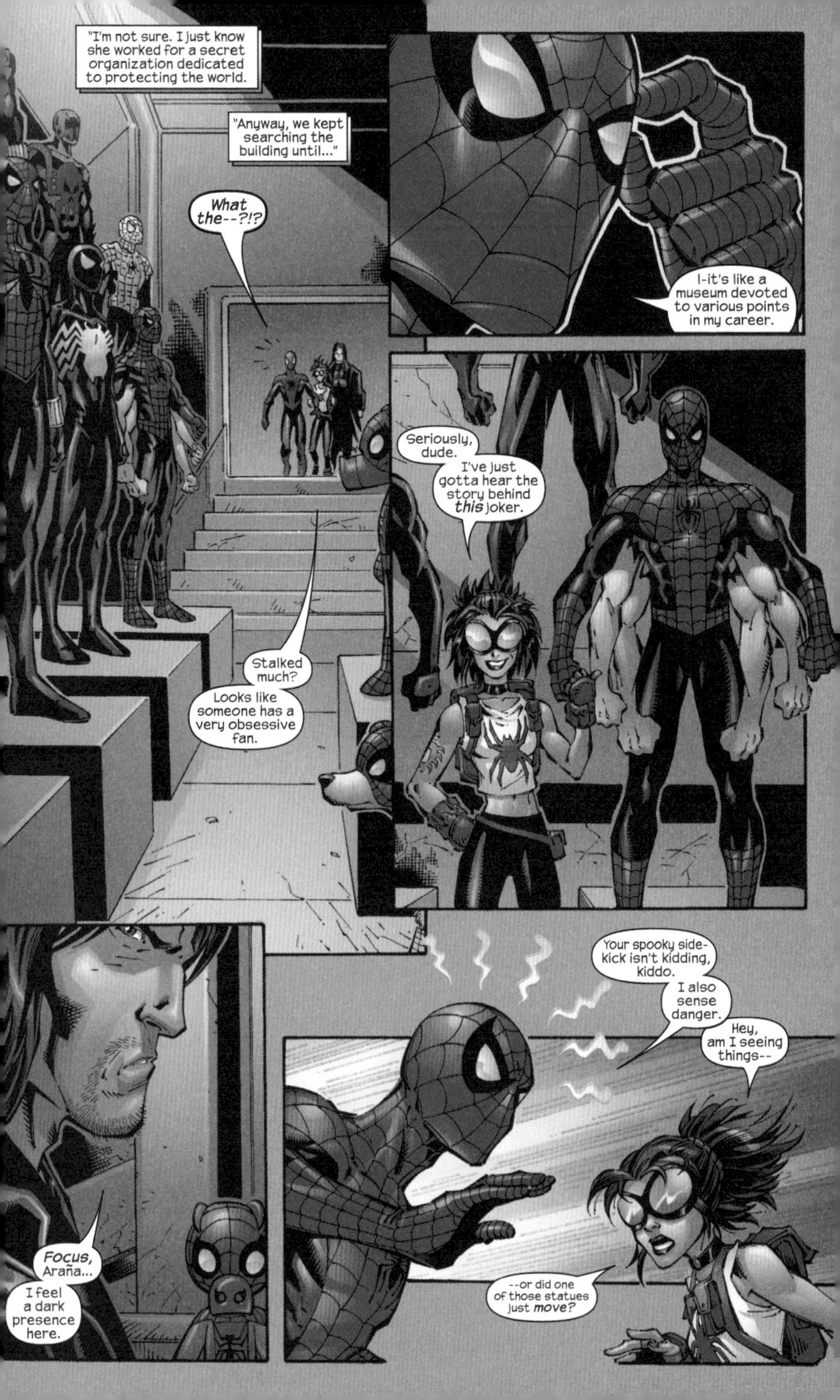
"I'm not sure. I just know she worked for a secret organization dedicated to protecting the world.
"Anyway, we kept searching the building until..."
What the--?!?
Stalked much?
Looks like someone has a very obsessive fan.
I-it's like a museum devoted to various points in my career.
Seriously, dude.
I've just gotta hear the story behind *this* joker.
Focus, Araña...
I feel a dark presence here.
Your spooky side-kick isn't kidding, kiddo.
I also sense danger.
Hey, am I seeing things--
--or did one of those statues just *move?*

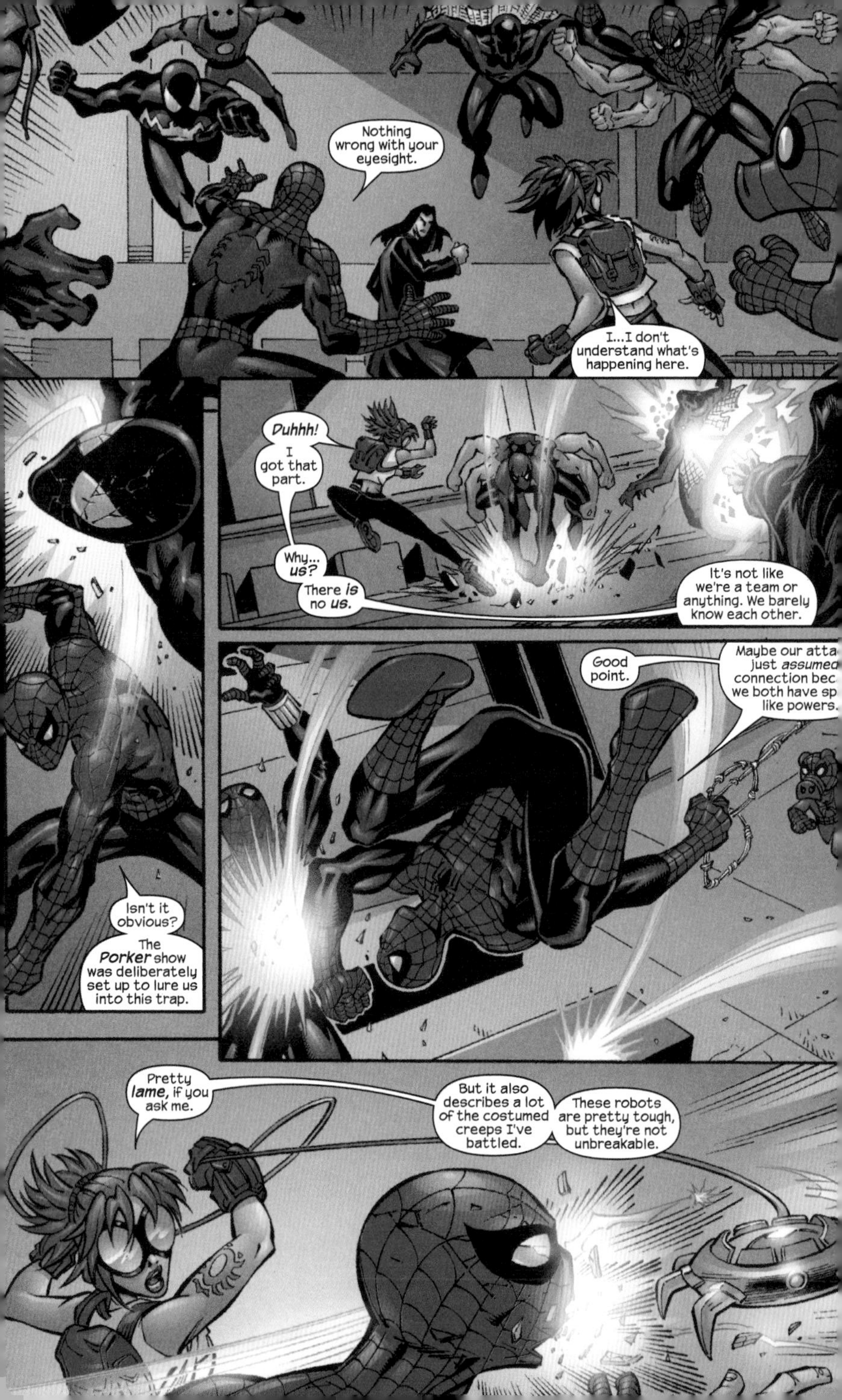
Nothing wrong with your eyesight.
I...I don't understand what's happening here.
Duhhh! I got that part.
Why... us? There is no us.
It's not like we're a team or anything. We barely know each other.
Isn't it obvious?
The Porker show was deliberately set up to lure us into this trap.
Good point.
Maybe our atta just assumed connection bec we both have sp like powers.
Pretty lame, if you ask me.
But it also describes a lot of the costumed creeps I've battled.
These robots are pretty tough, but they're not unbreakable.

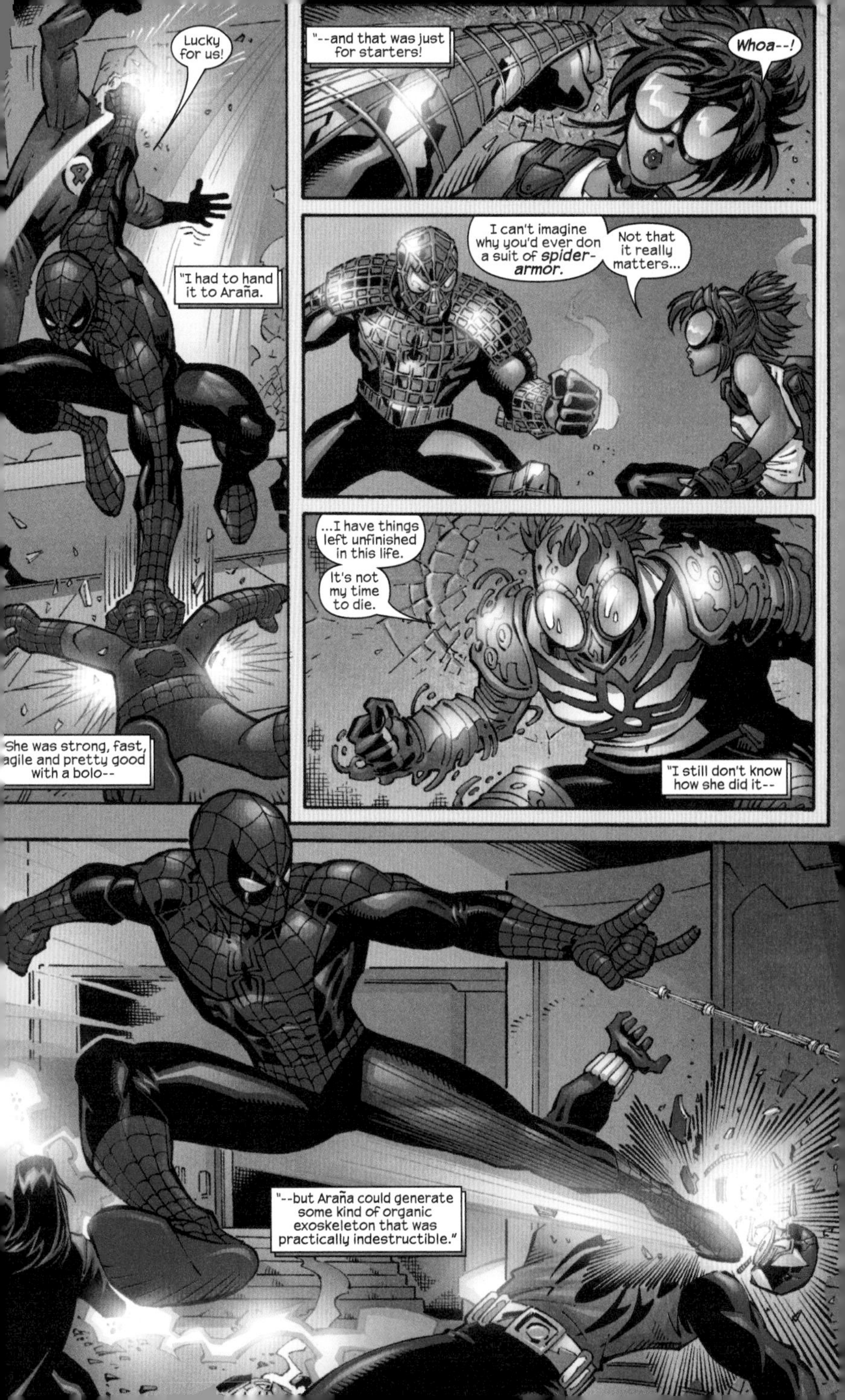

Lucky for us!
"I had to hand it to Araña.
She was strong, fast, agile and pretty good with a bolo--
"--and that was just for starters!
Whoa--!
I can't imagine why you'd ever don a suit of *spider-armor.*
Not that it really matters...
...I have things left unfinished in this life.
It's not my time to die.
"I still don't know how she did it--
"--but Araña could generate some kind of organic exoskeleton that was practically indestructible."

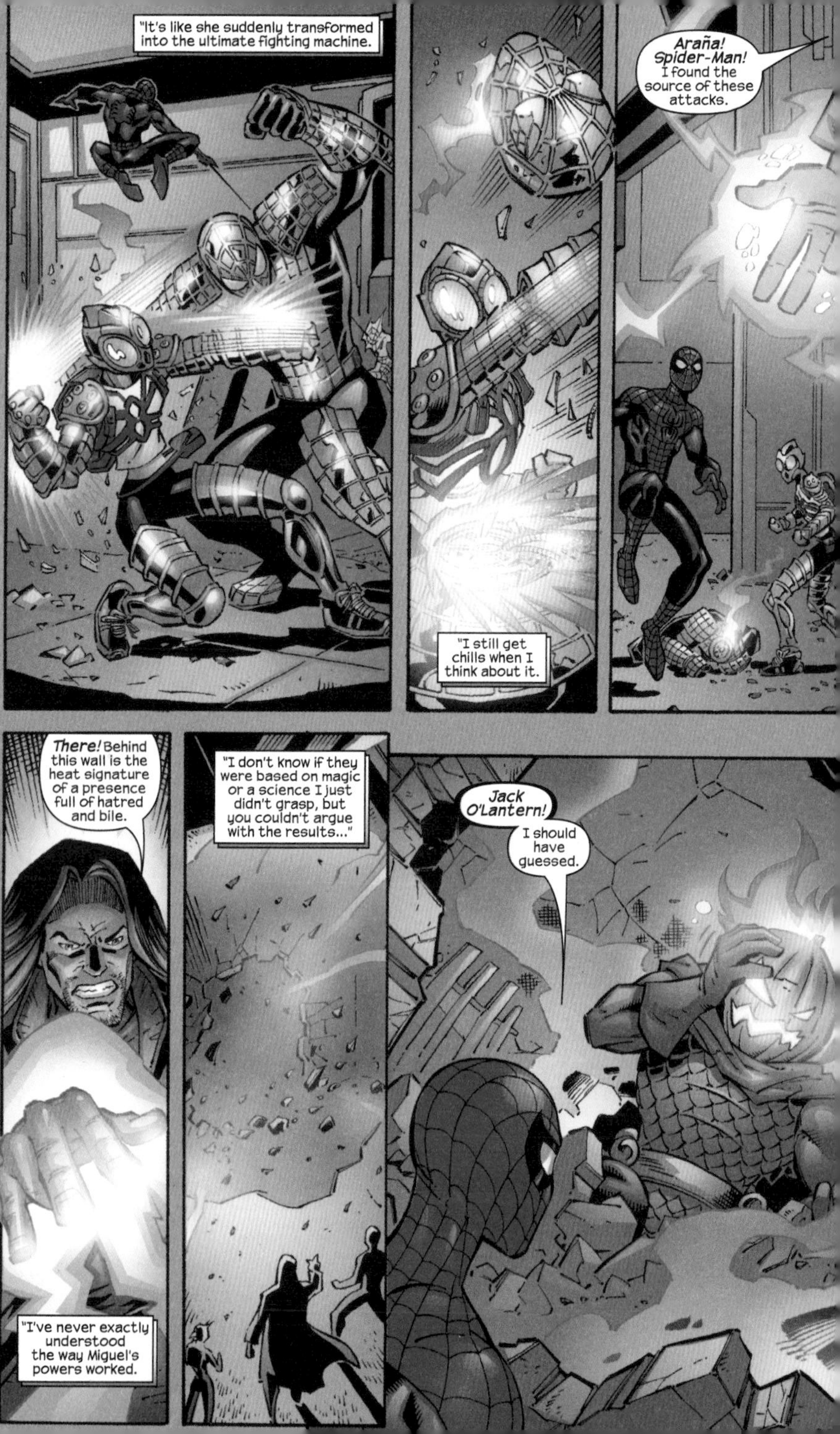
"It's like she suddenly transformed into the ultimate fighting machine.
"I still get chills when I think about it.
Araña! Spider-Man! I found the source of these attacks.
There! Behind this wall is the heat signature of a presence full of hatred and bile.
"I've never exactly understood the way Miguel's powers worked.
"I don't know if they were based on magic or a science I just didn't grasp, but you couldn't argue with the results..."
Jack O'Lantern! I should have guessed.

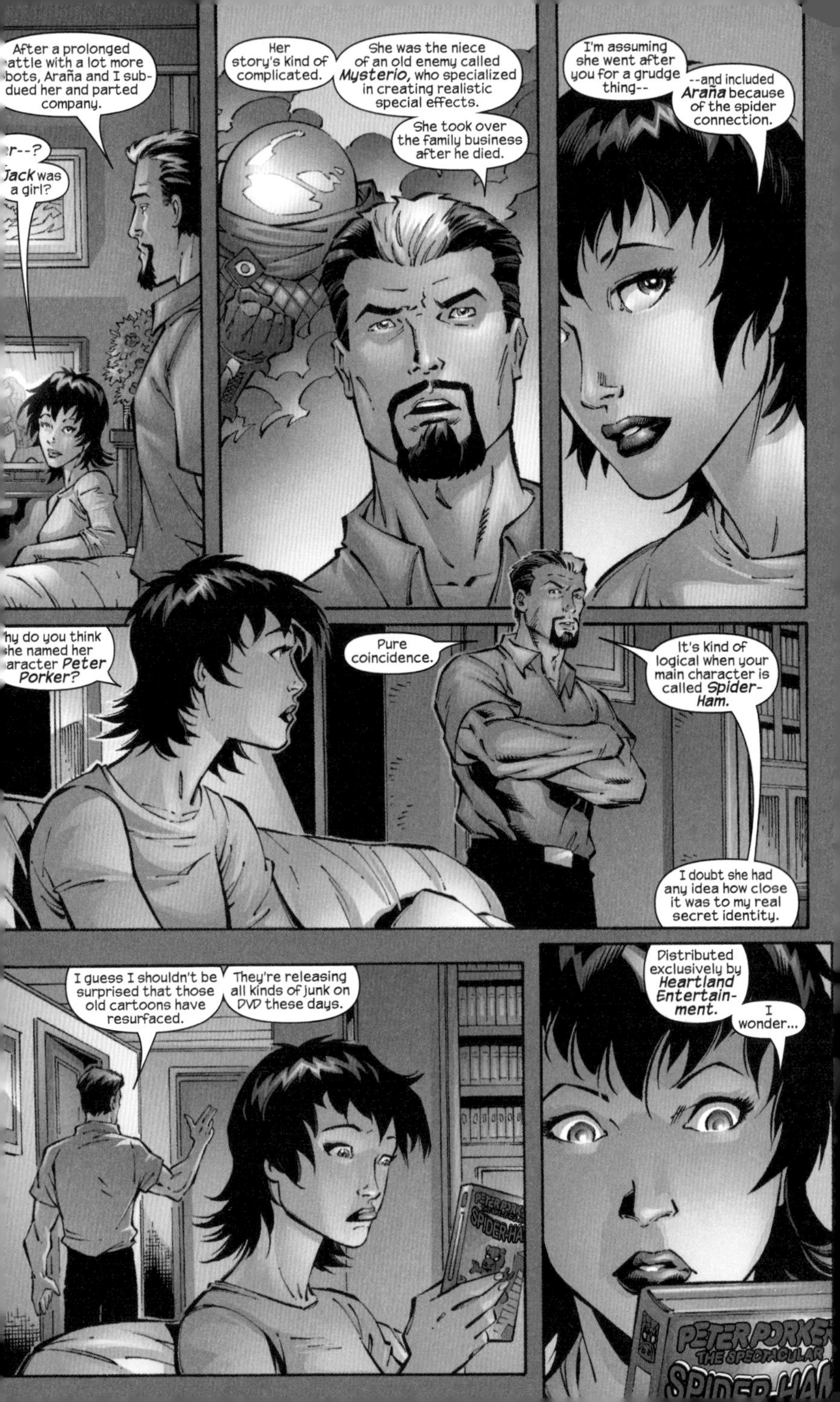
After a prolonged
attle with a lot more
bots, Araña and I sub-
dued her and parted
company.
r--?
Jack was
a girl?
Her
story's kind of
complicated.
She was the niece
of an old enemy called
Mysterio, who specialized
in creating realistic
special effects.
She took over
the family business
after he died.
I'm assuming
she went after
you for a grudge
thing--
--and included
Araña because
of the spider
connection.
hy do you think
he named her
aracter Peter
Porker?
Pure
coincidence.
It's kind of
logical when your
main character is
called Spider-
Ham.
I doubt she had
any idea how close
it was to my real
secret identity.
I guess I shouldn't be
surprised that those
old cartoons have
resurfaced.
They're releasing
all kinds of junk on
DVD these days.
Distributed
exclusively by
Heartland
Entertain-
ment.
I
wonder...
PETER PORKER
THE SPECTACULAR
SPIDER-HAM

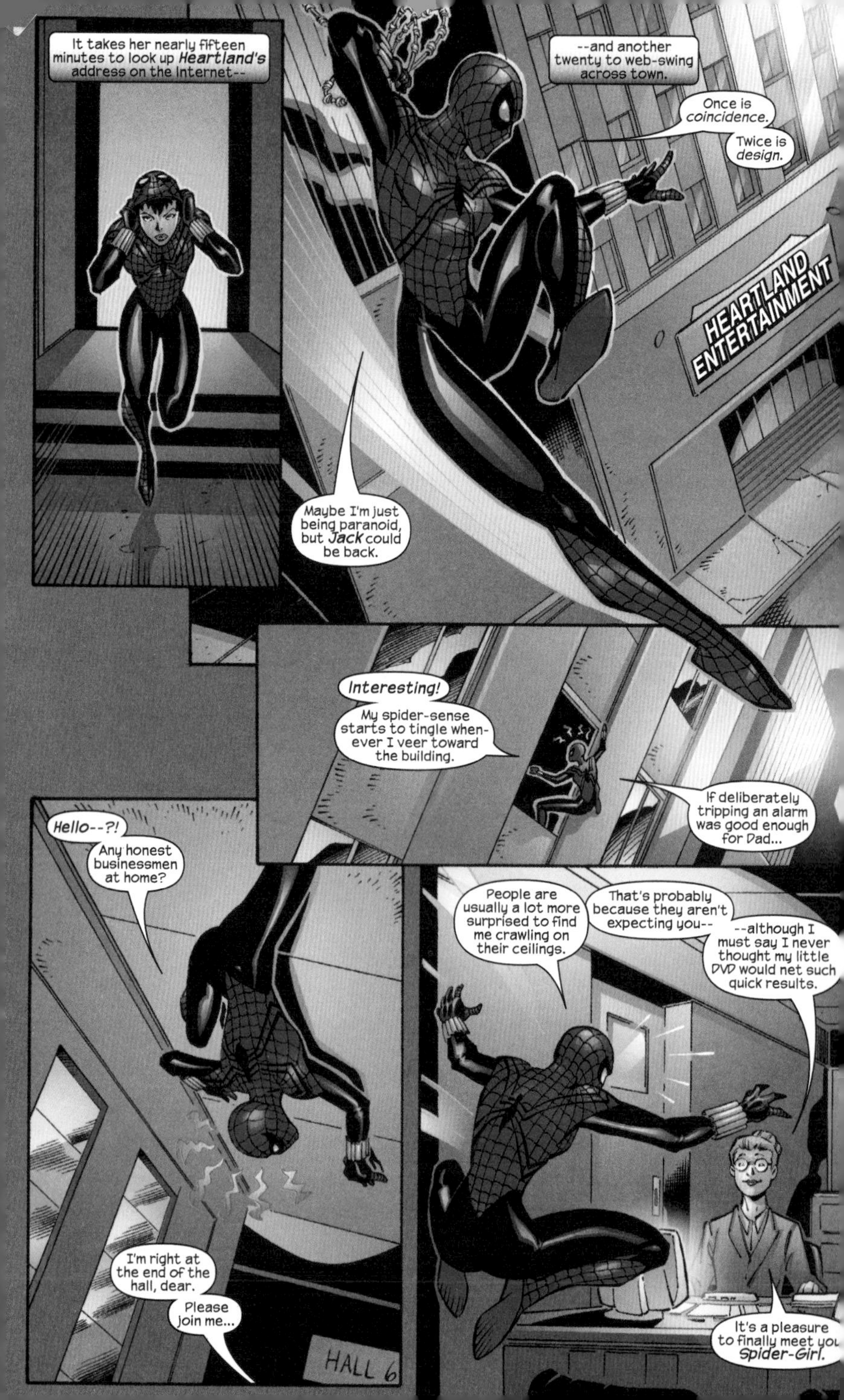

It takes her nearly fifteen minutes to look up Heartland's address on the Internet--
--and another twenty to web-swing across town.
Once is coincidence.
Twice is design.
HEARTLAND ENTERTAINMENT
Maybe I'm just being paranoid, but Jack could be back.
Interesting!
My spider-sense starts to tingle whenever I veer toward the building.
If deliberately tripping an alarm was good enough for Dad...
Hello--?!
Any honest businessmen at home?
I'm right at the end of the hall, dear.
Please join me...
HALL 6
People are usually a lot more surprised to find me crawling on their ceilings.
That's probably because they aren't expecting you--
--although I must say I never thought my little DVD would net such quick results.
It's a pleasure to finally meet you Spider-Girl.

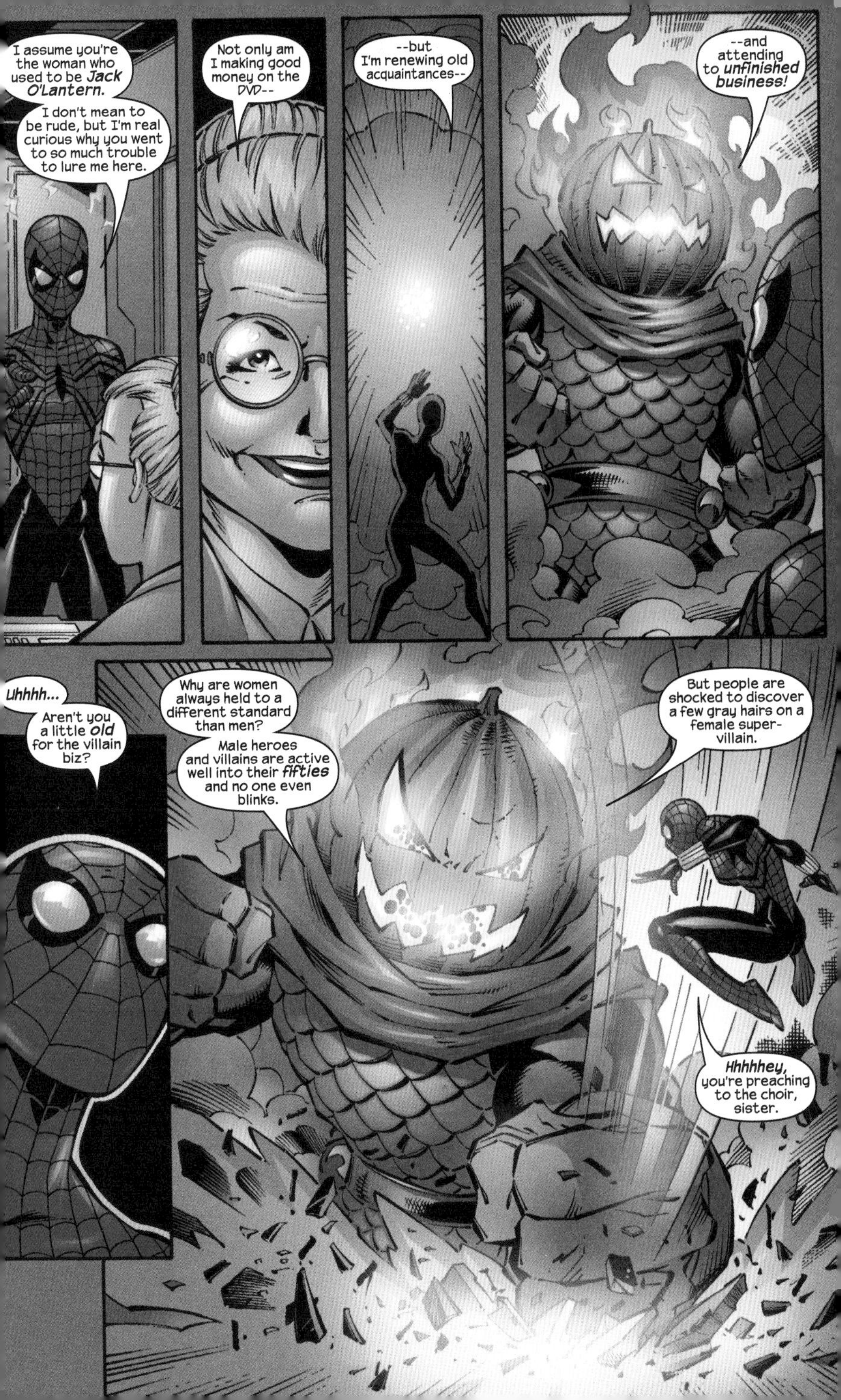

I assume you're the woman who used to be *Jack O'Lantern.*
I don't mean to be rude, but I'm real curious why you went to so much trouble to lure me here.
Not only am I making good money on the DVD--
--but I'm renewing old acquaintances--
--and attending to *unfinished business!*
Uhhhh...
Aren't you a little *old* for the villain biz?
Why are women always held to a different standard than men?
Male heroes and villains are active well into their *fifties* and no one even blinks.
But people are shocked to discover a few gray hairs on a female super-villain.
Hhhhhey, you're preaching to the choir, sister.

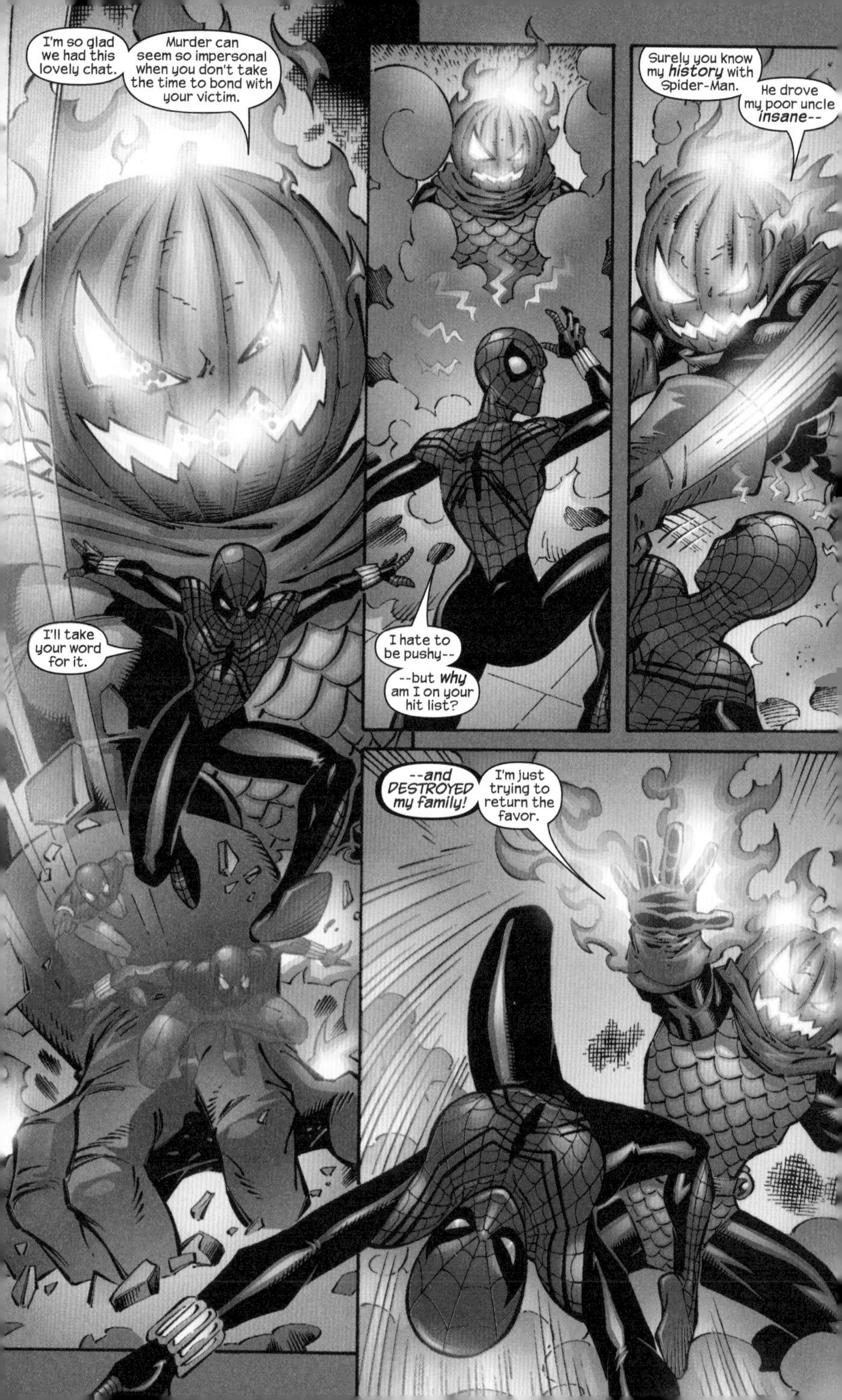
I'm so glad we had this lovely chat.
Murder can seem so impersonal when you don't take the time to bond with your victim.
I'll take your word for it.
I hate to be pushy--
--but *why* am I on your hit list?
Surely you know my *history* with Spider-Man.
He drove my poor uncle *insane*--
--*and DESTROYED my family!*
I'm just trying to return the favor.

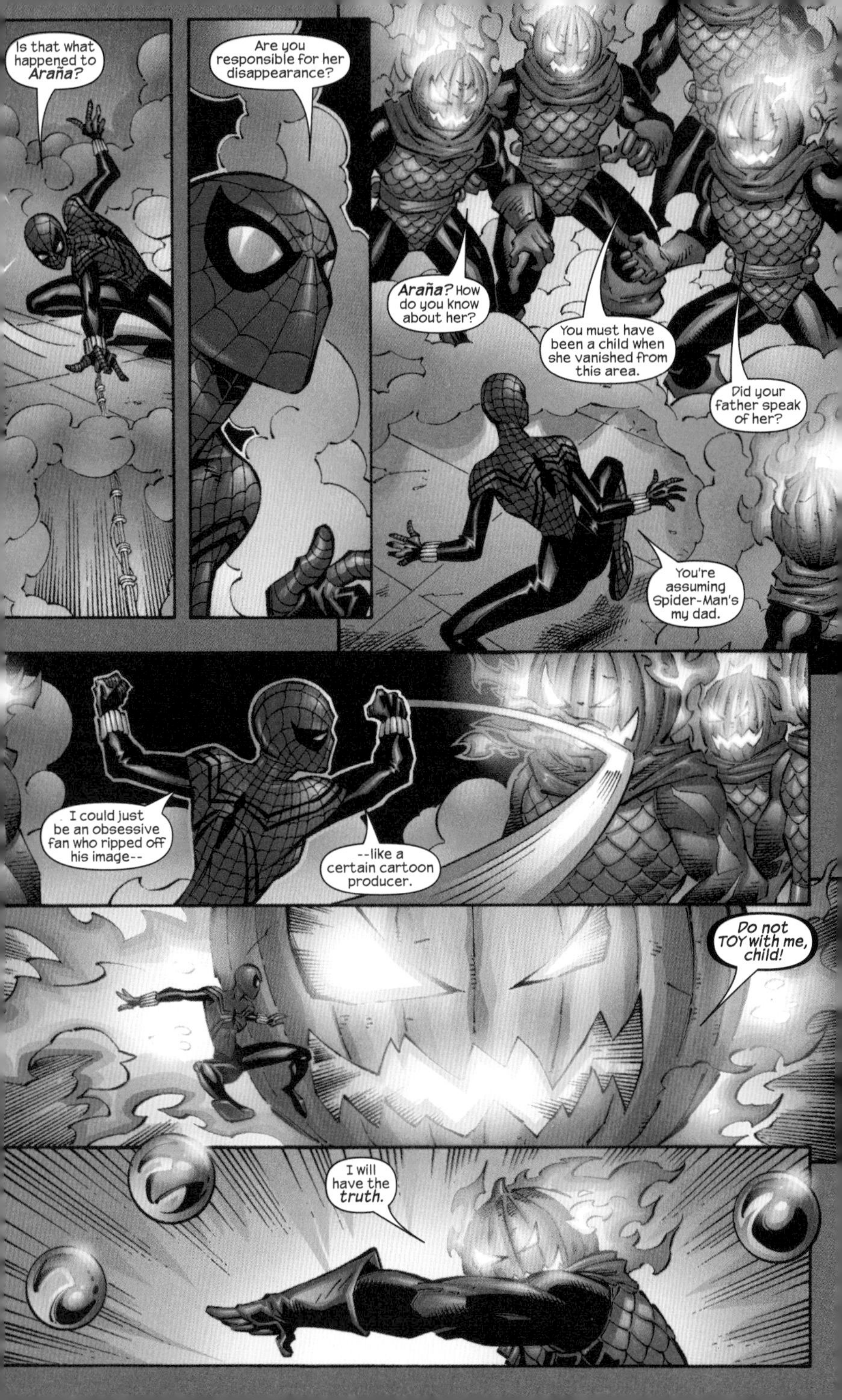
Is that what happened to *Araña*?
Are you responsible for her disappearance?
Araña? How do you know about her?
You must have been a child when she vanished from this area.
Did your father speak of her?
You're assuming Spider-Man's my dad.
I could just be an obsessive fan who ripped off his image--
--like a certain cartoon producer.
Do not TOY with me, child!
I will have the *truth.*

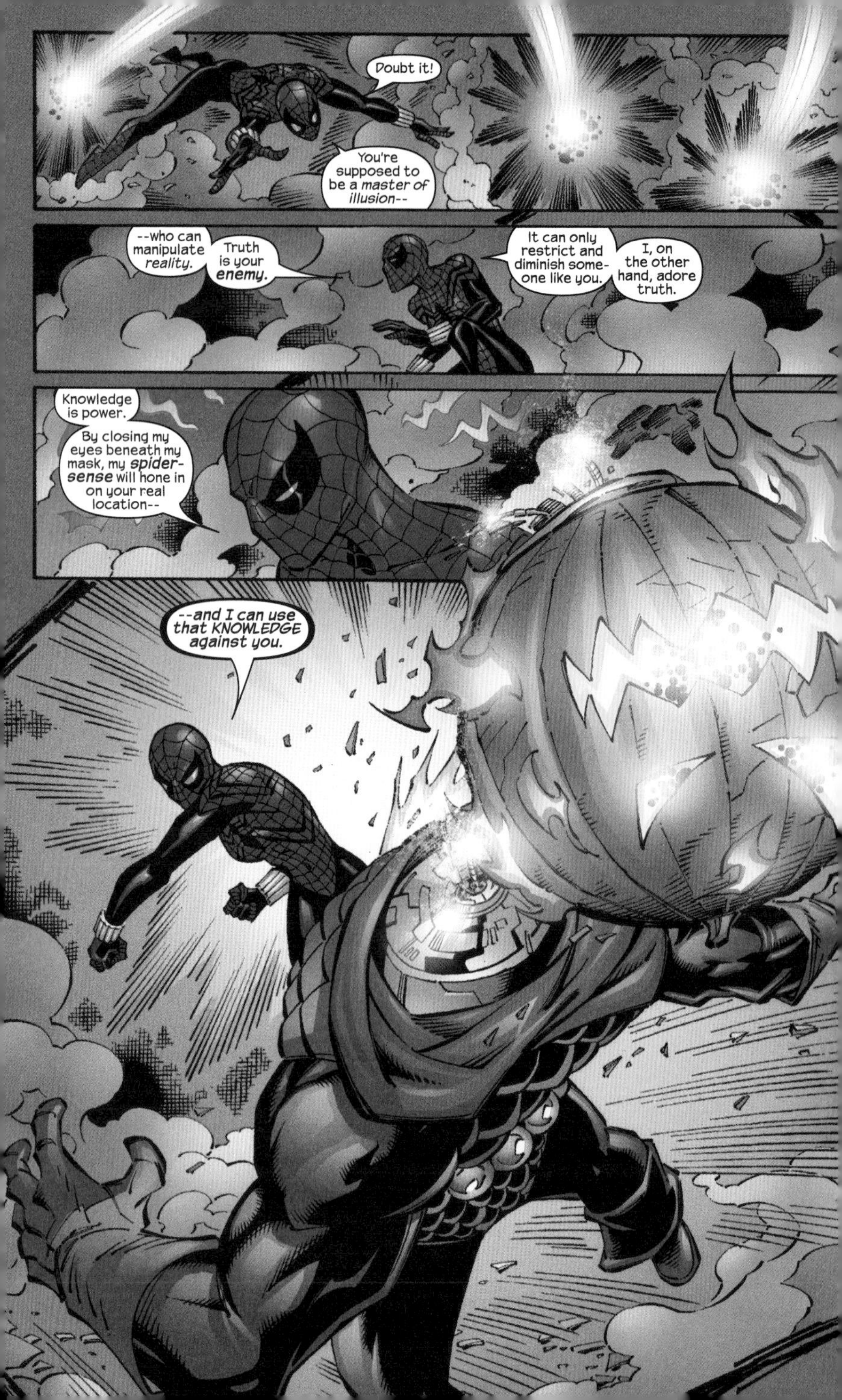

Doubt it!
You're supposed to be a *master of illusion*--
--who can manipulate *reality.*
Truth is your ***enemy.***
It can only restrict and diminish someone like you.
I, on the other hand, adore truth.
Knowledge is power.
By closing my eyes beneath my mask, my ***spider-sense*** will hone in on your real location--
--and I can use that KNOWLEDGE against you.

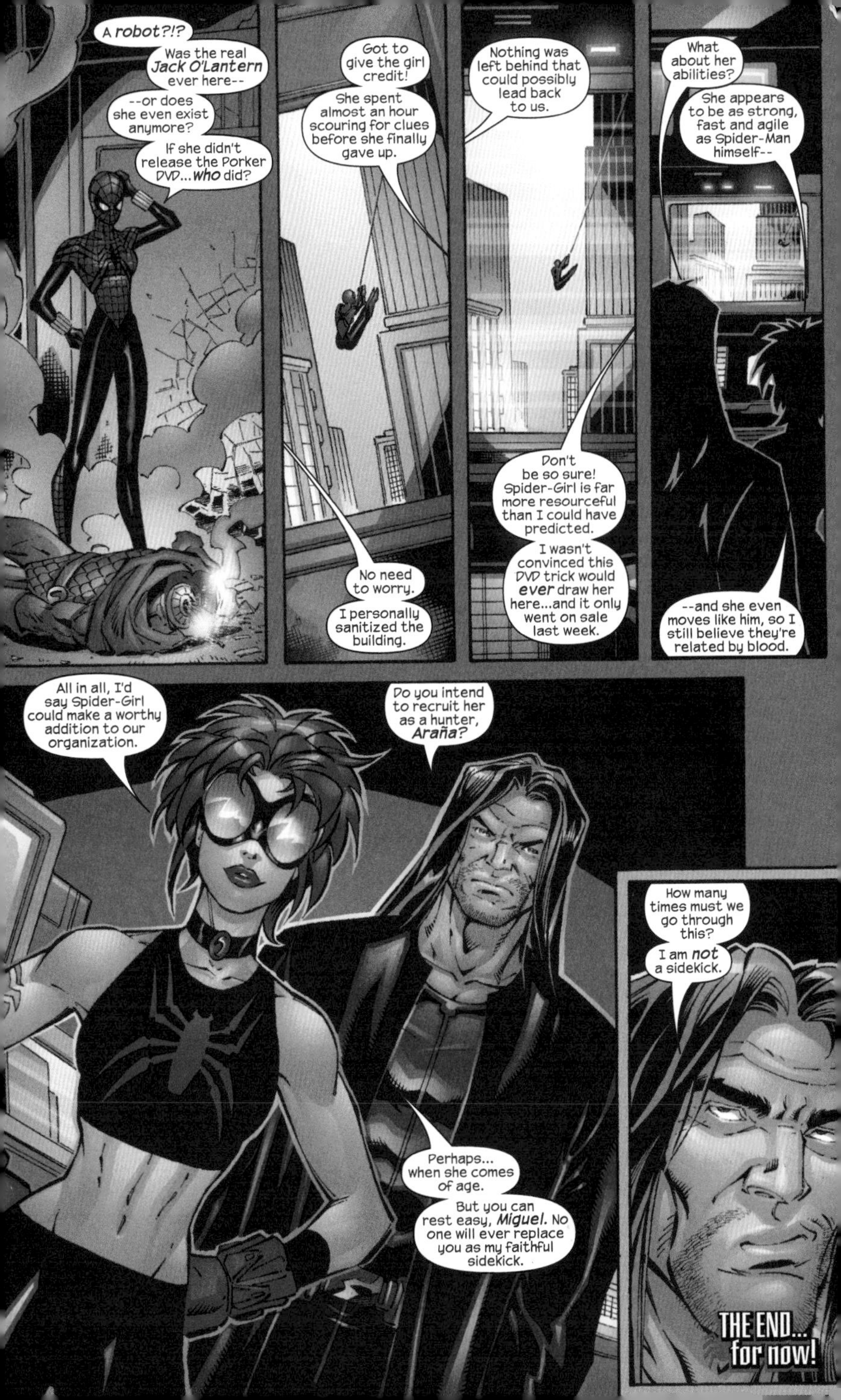

A robot?!?
Was the real Jack O'Lantern ever here--
--or does she even exist anymore?
If she didn't release the Porker DVD...who did?
Got to give the girl credit!
She spent almost an hour scouring for clues before she finally gave up.
No need to worry.
I personally sanitized the building.
Nothing was left behind that could possibly lead back to us.
Don't be so sure! Spider-Girl is far more resourceful than I could have predicted.
I wasn't convinced this DVD trick would ever draw her here...and it only went on sale last week.
What about her abilities?
She appears to be as strong, fast and agile as Spider-Man himself--
--and she even moves like him, so I still believe they're related by blood.
All in all, I'd say Spider-Girl could make a worthy addition to our organization.
Do you intend to recruit her as a hunter, Araña?
Perhaps... when she comes of age.
But you can rest easy, Miguel. No one will ever replace you as my faithful sidekick.
How many times must we go through this?
I am not a sidekick.
THE END... for now!

the AMAZING SPIDER-GIRL

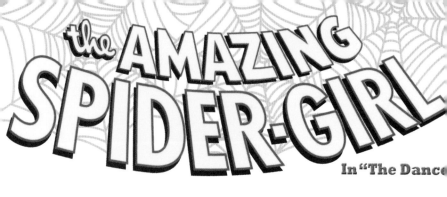

In “The Dance

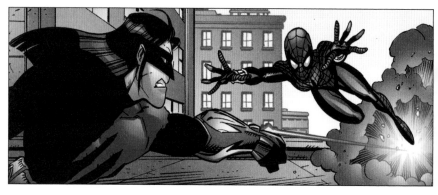

Story by Tom DeFalco
Art by Ron Lim, Scott Koblish and Avalon’s Rob Ro

I hurled myself backward to avoid the first stun grenade, somersaulting between two buildings that stood five stories along Queens Boulevard. As I plummeted toward the ground, I instinctively hit the trigger in the palm of my hand, tapping it twice in rapid succession as if it were a computer’s mouse. A thin cable-like strand of webbing squirted from the spinneret mechanism attached to my wrist. The strand glued itself to a nearby window ledge, saving me from becoming a sidewalk splat. I barely had time to catch my breath when a familiar tingling sensation advised me of more trouble. I’ve never figured out how this sensation actually works. I just know that I call it my spider-sense and it somehow warns me of danger. It’s one of the spider-like powers I inherited from my dad. My name is May “Mayday” Parker, and I am the daughter of Spider-Man. Of course, all things being equal, I’d like to think I’m better known as the amazing Spider-Girl.

Maybe I should have started at the beginning. I got up bright (well, kind of) and early (in a manner of speaking) on Saturday. I had promised my friend Davida Kirby that I’d help her decorate the school gym for tonight’s dance. My job was to swing by Emilio's Party Paradise, pick up our pre-ordered decorations and join the rest of the gang at Midtown High.

My late start got even later when I volunteered to feed my baby brother his breakfast and ended up wearing most of it. After a second shower and a change of outfit, I was finally ready to face the day.

I slipped into my Spider-Girl costume to make up for lost time and started web-swinging toward Emilio's. That's when my spider-sense first started tingling. Using it like a Geiger counter, I veered a couple of blocks out of my way. As I homed in on the source of the trouble, I caught sight of an old friend running across the rooftops. He calls himself Claw and claims to be the world's greatest cat burglar. He also considers himself quite the ladies' man. He was dressed in a black jumpsuit that sported a large crimson claw. It covered his left shoulder, spreading down to his abdomen. He's actually kind of cute in a "young Keanu Reeves first Matrix movie" kind of way. But talk about nerve! He once took time out from a battle to flirt with some women passing by. What am I-- chopped liver?!

I figured he was either returning from a heist or casing his next one. Either way, he wasn't up to any good. He wasn't exactly happy to see me either.

"Spider-Girl, my dear, it would be simply wonderful to catch up with you," he said as he extended his left gauntlet and fired that first stun grenade. "But I have a prior commitment."

"Why are you out so early?" I asked as I used my webbing to swing toward him. Two more stun grenades blasted toward me as I used my forward momentum to hurl myself skyward and out of their path.

"A gentleman never tells," he said. "However, if you must know, I'm meeting a very delightful companion for brunch."

I tucked into a barrel roll that angled me toward the rooftop where Claw stood. His eyes widened beneath his mask as I darted toward him.

"I would invite you along, but you have no idea how insecure a supermodel can be," he said, and fired two more stun grenades in my direction.

Though I was already in midair, I still managed to dodge the first one. I wasn't as lucky with the second. It caught me in the stomach, releasing enough force to hammer me into the roof and send me skidding out of control until I slammed to a stop against a not-so-convenient chimney.

I don't know if I lost consciousness or exactly what happened after that. The next thing I remembered was hearing a ringing in my ears. At first I thought it was a result of the stun grenade, but quickly realized it was my cell phone. Claw was long gone.

My cell phone continued to ring until I detached it from its holder on my web-shooters. Davida was on the line, and she wasn't happy.

"You were supposed to be here by now," she said, making no attempt to mask her exasperation.

"I ran into an old friend and I lost track of time," I said. "I should arrive at the gym in the next ten or so minutes."

🕷 🕷 🕷

It actually took sixteen. Not bad when you consider that I had to slip out of costume, switch into my civilian clothes, wait on line at Emilio's and jog the five blocks to Midtown High while carrying a carton full of decorations. (My spider-like strength and endurance comes in very handy at the oddest times!)

Instead of greeting me with open arms, Davida ripped the carton from me, pulled open the box and stared at the contents with growing alarm.

"You picked up the wrong order," she said.

"No, I didn't. This is the one Emilio gave me, and the label says

Midtown High."

"But our school colors are orange and white. These decorations are silver and black," she said.

"I changed them," Simone DeSantos announced as she swept over to us. Simone believes she was born to be the center of everyone's attention and there are no exceptions to the rule. She had recently lost her bid for student council president to Davida and still resented it.

"Orange and white are dull. Nobody looks good against them," Simone said. "Silver and black are much more elegant and sophisticated."

"Simone," Davida said, as if she were speaking to a small child. "The school colors are orange and white. The decoration committee voted on orange and white. You were supposed to order orange and white."

"I did what I thought was right," Simone said. "Initiative should be ewarded. Any good leader knows that."

The old Davida probably would have decked her at this point. (Heck, I don't believe violence ever solves anything and I wanted to deck her.) However, ever since she became student council president, Davida has given up her old steamrolling ways. She no longer tramples everyone in her path. She now plays the politician and tries to convince them to join her team. If that fails, then she flips into trample mode.

Realizing that further conversation with Simone would only be an exercise in futility, Davida whipped out her cell phone and called Emilio's. He immediately agreed to exchange our order. Unfortunately, orange wasn't exactly a huge seller and he didn't have much white, either. He just couldn't supply us with enough balloons and decorations in the proper colors. Otherwise, he'd be glad to help.

"I guess that's that," Simone said cheerfully.

Davida thanked Emilio, closed her phone, narrowed her eyes and took a step toward Simone. When in doubt, go with decking.

Holding a stack of papers, Courtney Duran suddenly inserted herself between Davida and Simone. "I need to talk to you about the tickets, Davida. There seems to be a computer glitch," she said.

"Can't this wait? I'm kind of busy right now," Davida said.

"Instead of printing paper tickets, we went the e-route and listed all the buyers on the computer," Courtney explained patiently. "We're going to have some pretty unhappy students if we can't find their names."

Davida glared at Courtney, who responded with a hopeful smile. Courtney is one of my oldest and dearest friends. She's a head shorter than me, but has a lot more heart. Her friendship is unshakable and unconditional.

I quickly realized that Courtney was only trying to prevent bloodshed. So did Davida on some unconscious level. Shaking her head in disgust, she made a vague gesture in the general vicinity of the decorations as she walked off without another word.

"I knew Davida would eventually agree with me," Simone said as soon as she was out of earshot. "It's so much better when everyone does."

"It's not like she had much choice," I mumbled as I continued to weigh the pros and cons of decking her.

"There's always a choice. Mine or the wrong one," Simone said. "I wish I could stay and help, but I'm due at the hair stylist. I'm sure you'll all do a wonderful job."

"You're leaving?" I asked.

Jimmy Yama, Heather Noble and Wes Westin immediately surrounded me.

"Why don't we work as a team?" Jimmy suggested and took me by the arm. Jimmy is an old friend who used to hide his insecurities behind sarcasm. He once had a bit of a crush on me, but it was strictly one-sided. My loss! Jimmy's one of the nicest guys I know. He had the worst luck with girls until he somehow linked up with Heather. She's pretty, popular and is lucky enough to see something in Jimmy that I never did. They make an odd but endearing couple. Wes is Jimmy's friend and the school artist, the guy that students and teachers call when they need a spot illustration for a flyer or the school newspaper.

I picked up a handful of decorations, turned and almost collided with Meagyn Brady. She's a little mouse of a girl who seems to share a lot of my classes, but I honestly couldn't tell you which ones. Meagyn isn't the type of person you notice. It's almost like she blends in with the background.

"Sorry, Meagyn," I said. "I didn't even realize you were on the decoration committee."

"I'm not," she said. "But I want to help."

"We could use it." We only had a few hours to decorate the entire gym, a lot less time than usual. We normally would have started right after the last class on Friday. Unfortunately, the basketball team had a night game and we had to wait until this morning. Yeah, it would be a major hassle to finish the job in time, but sometimes you just have to take one for the team.

🕷 🕷 🕷

I climbed the nearest ladder and got down to work, but I had more than decorations on my mind. I kept thinking about Claw and wondering what he'd been doing when I first stumbled across him. I was beginning to doubt that he was returning from a heist. If he was planning one, I still had a chance to stop him. Scratch that! I had a responsibility to stop him. It would be my fault if anyone was hurt or injured when he actually pulled the job.

My family is big on responsibility. When my dad first got his powers from an accidental encounter with a radioactive spider, he planned to go into show business and make his fortune. He soon learned that people with great power have a responsibility to use that power wisely. He did. As the amazing Spider-Man, he became one of the most famous and respected heroes of the modern age. His career spanned over a decade, but was cut short when he lost a leg in a desperate battle with one of his enemies. Even that didn't stop Dad for long. He continued his crusade against crime by becoming a forensic scientist and began working for the Midtown Police Department.

was so proud when I first learned about Dad's past. I became even prouder when I realized that I had inherited his powers and could continue his legacy. That's another reason why I was haunted by Claw. I'm not the only one who looks bad when I fail. It also reflects on Dad. Claw never would have escaped him!

I was still trying to figure out how to get a line on Claw when I suddenly realized that someone was talking to me.

"You okay up there, May? You're looking a little weird," Wes said.

I was standing on one of the larger stepladders, attaching silver streamers and black balloons to the underside of the basketball backboard.

"Sorry, Wes. I must have been daydreaming. I have to be here because Davida would kill me if I wasn't. How'd you get roped into this madness?"

"I came as a favor to Jimmy. I guess Courtney recruited Heather and she drafted him. He called me because he didn't want to be the only guy on the committee. He even conned me into volunteering to help clean up after the dance."

"Guess I'll see you there."

"I guess," Wes said, suddenly fascinated with his shoes. He seemed to take a breath before he continued, "You going to dance with anyone?"

"Not me," I said, stretching to get one last streamer in place. "I'll be at the ticket table with Courtney most of the night. Didn't seem fair to inflict that on a date."

At least that was my story. The truth was a little more complicated. I wasn't really seeing anyone at the moment. My last relationship had ended recently and badly. Who am I kidding? That's how they all end. I was beginning to doubt my ability to pick a decent guy. Besides, between my studies and web-swinging, who had time for boyfriends?

I looked down and realized that Wes's gaze had returned to his shoes. They were an old pair of cross-trainers. They seemed nice enough, but hardly worth such attention. Maybe his feet hurt.

"Hand me a few black streamers," I said.

"Sure," he said with a pronounced lack of enthusiasm.

Yeah, I thought, the poor guy must be in a lot of pain.

We eventually finished the job, and I have to say the silver and black didn't look too bad. Not that I'd ever admit it to Simone. Not even under extreme torture.

"See you later," Wes said tentatively.

"Yeah," I said as I headed home. I

had finally figured out what to do about Claw. I'd call my Uncle Phil.

Phil Urich isn't a real blood relation. He's even better, a family friend who's been working in the police lab alongside my dad for as long as I remember. I knew he'd drawn the weekend shift and would be more than happy to lend me a hand.

"What do you want this time?"

"Is that any way to greet your favorite niece?"

"If you're playing the niece card, it must be something big," he said before adding, "Something you want me to keep from your parents."

"Cynicism doesn't become you, Uncle Phil," I said and told him about Claw. "I've got a hunch he was prepping a job. Could you see if there are any likely targets along or bordering that stretch of Queens Boulevard?"

"I'll get back to you," he said with a sigh, "but I'm not going to lie for you."

"Of course not! You can tell my parents the absolute truth," I said, "if they specifically ask about Claw."

He muttered something that I'm sure I misheard. Uncle Phil didn't use that kind of language. And certainly not to me!

🕷 🕷 🕷

A handful of strained peas hit me above the right eye. It matched the one dripping down the front of my shirt.

Benjy giggled, proud of scoring another direct hit.

"You want me to take him?" my mother asked.

"Nope," I said. "We're having a good time."

Mom arched an eyebrow as she looked me over. A pretty girl looks good in almost anything. Strained peas may be the exception.

"Shouldn't you be getting ready for the dance?" she asked.

"I'd rather spend time with my favorite guy," I said, puffing out my cheeks and bulging my eyes to draw another giggle from Benjy.

I knew Mom was disappointed that I didn't have a date. According to everything I heard, she was very popular in high school. The former

Mary Jane Watson loved school dances and was crowned the queen of many of them. My parents have often told me how they first met and I'm still amazed--and thankful--they ever got together. I sometimes wonder if they were the Tommy and Heather of their day.

When Ben tried to wear his dinner plate as a hat, I turned him over to Mom and headed upstairs for a shower. I slipped into my favorite cerulean blue dress, a spaghetti-wrapped affair that ended a few inches above my knees. My shoes had been dyed a matching blue. I was blasting away with my hair dryer when I heard a tentative knock at the door.

Dad entered my room and looked me over, his face warring between pride and sheer terror. He was happy to hear I was going stag. It's kind of ironic when you think about it. He seemed fine with me donning a costume and battling super-menaces, but grew positively pale whenever I went out on a date.

"You okay, kid? You seemed a little distracted at dinner."

I smiled, planning to keep my run-in with Claw to myself. It wasn't like I intended to pursue the matter. How could I? I had a dance to attend, a gym to clean up afterwards and very little chance of running across my favorite cat burglar. There was no need to burden my dad. But I had lied to him in the past and never liked the results. I told him everything, even mentioning my call to Uncle Phil and my belief that I would be responsible if Claw injured anyone on his next job.

"You can't think that way," Dad said.

"Why not?" I said. "You always did."

He looked a little surprised by my response, but didn't argue the point. He merely smiled and said, "You don't have to worry about Claw. Just enjoy the dance."

🕷 🕷 🕷

The DJ seemed to have a thing for female pop vocalists and contemporary rap. He had fallen into a predictable pattern of alternating between the two genres. I didn't really care. I was sitting out in the lobby with Courtney. We were stationed behind a large table and armed with our lists. Students would present their ID cards. We would locate their names on our e-lists or charge them for their tickets. The process was swift and relatively painless...

...until Simone arrived.

Her makeup was flawless and her hair done to perfection. She wore a floor-length, candy-apple-red sheath that looked like she had been poured into it. She looked absolutely gorgeous and I just wanted to kill her.

"I like your dress, Parker," she said.

"I wore something similar when I graduated grade school."

Nope, killing was too good for her. She demanded torture and maiming. Lots and lots of maiming!

"There seems to be a problem," Courtney said, as she ran her finger down the page before her. "Your name should be on this list, but I can't seem to find it."

"Try checking it with your eyes open, Duran," Simone said. "I paid for my ticket the first day they went on sale."

Courtney studied the sheet in front of her and reached for another. "Sorry, you're not here."

"This is ridiculous. Someone obviously made a mistake," Simone said, her eyes boring into the top of Courtney's head. "Fix it! I'm missing the dance."

"I'm sure your name's on the master list. Why don't you come with me to the computer room and we can sort this all out?"

Simone seemed torn for a moment, not sure if she should make a bigger fuss or wait until she could lord it over Courtney for making a mistake. Lording won, and she followed with her head held high.

I handled the rest of the kids on line and was just putting the lists in alphabetical order when my cell

phone began buzzing in my purse. I pulled it out and slapped it again my ear.

"I think I found Claw's target," Uncle Phil said without preamble. "A armored car company gave the precinct a heads-up on a shipment of diamonds that's headed out to JFK tonight. They'll be taking the 59th Street Bridge to Queens Boulevard before hitting the parkways."

"Any idea when they'll reach our neighborhood?"

"Should be any minute now," he said. "You want backup?"

"Thanks for the offer, but I think I can handle a single cat burglar."

"Whatever," Phil said and disconnected.

I looked over my shoulder, hoping to see Courtney headed back to the table. No such luck. She was probably still going through the lists with Simone. Oh, well! I'd just have to sit here until they returned. The dance was in full swing. Most of the students had already arrived, but I couldn't leave the table unattended.

"You need a bathroom break?" Meagyn Brady asked. She had somehow snuck up behind me again. "I could watch the table while you're gone."

"That'd be great, Meagyn."

"Take your time," she said. "No one

ver asks me to dance, anyway."

"You're a lifesaver, Meagyn." In more ways than one!

trotted down the hallway as fast as could in two-inch stilettos--which was pretty fast, thanks to my spider-ke agility!

headed for the girl's locker room nd removed my backpack. One of he disadvantages of my costume is hat it rarely fits under my clothes. Luckily, there's more than enough oom for it in my backpack.

had already whipped off my dress nd donned most of my costume vhen my spider-sense suddenly started to tingle. Someone else was about to join me in the locker room.

"We're not supposed to be in here," a female voice whispered.

"We won't stay long," her male companion answered.

Kissing sounds soon filled the room. Hoping to make a getaway without being spotted, I pulled on my mask, stuffed my dress and shoes into my backpack and threw it over my shoulder. I used my ability to stick to any surface to crawl up the nearest wall. As I slithered across the ceiling toward the window, I glanced at the couple that was sucking face. I was surprised to recognize Jimmy and Heather. I suddenly regretted comparing them to my parents. The cor-responding image almost made me gag.

🕷 🕷 🕷

No words can adequately express the feeling one gets from web-swinging. You're stories above the ground, held aloft by a strand of gossamer-thin webbing. You ride that strand to the apex of its arc before hurtling yourself into the air as you fire and catch the next strand. And the next. Forget roller-coasters and other thrill rides. They're snoozers compared to web-singing.

I was approaching Queens Boulevard when I heard the explosion. It was soon followed by the screech of brakes and a loud crashing sound. A dark cloud of smoke mushroomed from the street, along with the acrid stench of burning debris.

Claw stood with a half-dozen armed men. They encircled two uniformed security men who knelt in the street in front of an armored car, which lay on its side like a dying animal. Its radiator grill had been torn open. The armed men were dressed in black jumpsuits, obviously modeled after Claw's. One of them carried a handheld rocket launcher. He was big, hairy and seemed proud to be disreputable. Claw was directing him toward the rear of the armored car when I arrived.

"Hurry! We have maybe five minutes before this place will be swarming with cops."

"I'm afraid the police are the least of your problems," I shouted as I exploded into the crowd, stunning two of the gunmen with swift kicks to their heads. I used my forward momentum to cartwheel to the street where I landed in one of my classic spider-like poses.

"You're really starting to annoy me, young lady," Claw said.

"You only have yourself to blame. You know I bill myself as a friendly neighborhood web-slinger. What part of 'neighborhood' don't you understand?"

Three of his henchmen sprang toward me. I swept my right leg out, tripping the lead man. As he pitched forward, I sprang from the ground and shoved him hard in the chest, sending him crashing into the other two.

"That's quite enough, Spider-Girl. If you don't surrender, these two security guards won't live to regret it."

I cut my eyes toward Claw. He and Disreputable had shifted their aim. The rocket launcher was now targeting the security guards.

Claw spoke in a low voice. "I'm a lover, not a fighter. I don't believe in violence and have no desire to harm anyone. I just want the jewels. Please don't force me to go against my nature! All you have to do is lie face down on the ground with your hands clasped behind your head.

My men and I will pop this tin can, take the gems and be on our merry way. Be a real hero and put these security guards and their families first."

I froze in place, closing my eyes beneath my mask. I hated the idea of placing myself at Claw's mercy. What choice did I have? I couldn't risk those poor men. No one is supposed to die on my watch! My only hope was to do as Claw asked and wait for an opening.

I gritted my teeth and slowly lowered myself to the ground.

"Move it, girlie!" Disreputable said. "We don't got all night."

The rocket launcher veered from the security guards and focused on me. This was the chance I'd been hoping for. I tensed, preparing to launch myself at him, fairly confident that I could avoid the oncoming blast.

My spider-like reflexes are about forty times faster than any Olympic athlete's. That's pretty darned fast. Not fast enough, apparently. Even before I could spring into action, a familiar voice said, "Be careful with that thing! You could put an eye out."

An equally familiar Thwippp! Followed, and Disreputable's eyes bulged as the rocket launcher was suddenly torn from his grasp and soared skyward, carried aloft by a strand of webbing.

Standing on a nearby rooftop was my dad, the always-amazing Spider-Man.

Claw and his gunman stared upward, unable to believe their eyes. Me, I was just glad I wear a full face mask so that no one could see the goofy smile on my face. I didn't know how Dad heard about this heist or why he came. I was just so happy to see him.

"You boys made an awful mess with that armored car. Why don't you join me up here where the air smells better?" Dad said, as he gently lay the rocket launcher on the roof. He paused before adding, "How rude of me! Since you can't crawl up walls or swing on webs, I'll have to come down to your level."

He cannonballed off the roof, ricocheted off the top of the armored car and bowled over a handful of the gunmen. Even though he wore an artificial leg, my dad was more than a match for Claw and his people. Obviously favoring his good leg, Dad pivoted and bounced forward.

"I hope you boys will be careful with me. I'm a little out of practice and I'd hate to bruise my delicate fists when I slam them against your rock-hard jaws." Two more gunmen hit the pavement.

Only Claw and Disreputable were left. As much as I enjoyed watch-ing Dad in action, I felt the need to contribute. Leaping for a nearby street lamp, I whirled around it to gain momentum and hurled my-self into the air. I tucked myself into a ball and bounced off Disreputable's head as he turned to flee. He stood completely still for a moment. A brief moment. Then his legs seemed to melt beneath him and he pitched sideways like a felled ox.

Slackjawed and shaken by the unexpected turn of events, Claw kept shifting his eyes from me to my father.

"As I said before, I'm a lover." He lowered himself to the street, putting his face down on the ground with his hands clasped behind his head and said, "Not a fighter."

As we hog-tied Claw and his men, I said to my father, "I assume you called my uncle."

"I did," Dad said. "I also talked this over with your mother, and we both thought you deserved a night off. Silly us."

"Silly me. I thought you were retired."

"I am," he said. "But I'm willing to make exceptions in your case."

Police sirens growled in the distance, growing louder and ever more insistent.

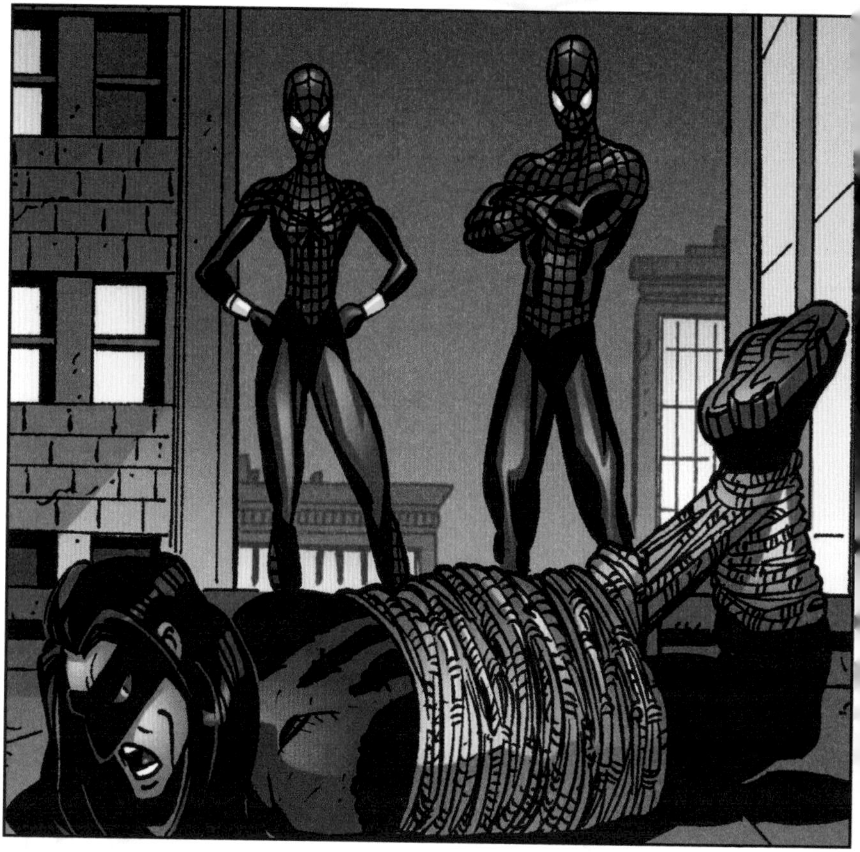

"Don't you have someplace to be?" my father said, and I just knew he was smiling beneath his mask.

🕷 🕷 🕷

I returned to Midtown High, retrieved my backpack and slipped into the girl's locker room. To my relief, I had the place to myself. I slithered back into my dress and spent another ten minutes working on my hair. If you think hat hair is bad, you've never experienced costume hair.

The ticket table was deserted and had been shut down long ago. I could hear the DJ wrapping up the evening. I stood at the entrance to the gym and peered at the crowd. There was no sign of Courtney, but Davida was standing with a few members of the cleanup committee. Jimmy and Heather were in their usual tight clench in the middle of the dance floor, completely oblivious to the fast music.

I was surprised to see Wes shaking it with Meagyn Brady. She wore the biggest smile I'd ever seen on her face. Something stirred at the pit of my stomach. Probably a late reaction to the strained peas. I was happy for Meagyn. Really.

As the song ended, the DJ announced the last dance. I saw Wes whisper something in Meagyn's ear. Her eyes sparkled as she looked toward me and gave me a little wave. She headed off to parts unknown and Wes ambled in my direction.

"Care to dance?" he asked.

"It would be a pleasure."

As he took my hand and began to lead me toward the dance floor, I heard a commotion behind us.

"You did this on purpose!" Simone shouted.

Courtney, doing her best imitation of a church mouse, slowly walked beside her. "Not my fault we got locked in the computer room."

"Oh, yeah? You deliberately made me miss the entire dance."

"Calm down, Simone." Davida said, rushing up to the two girls. "I'm sure we can solve this problem."

"HOW? She ruined everything! My dress would have looked just perfect against the silver and black decorations. Now that everyone has seen it, I can't possibly wear it again."

"That's a real shame," Davida said, her face completely devoid of expression. "Maybe you can get one that'll go with orange and white."

Simone glared at Davida, turned on her heels and stormed toward the exit.

"You got locked in the computer room?" Davida asked.

"Oops!" Courtney responded with a mischievous smile.

I didn't stick around to hear any more. Wes and I had a dance to finish.

THE END

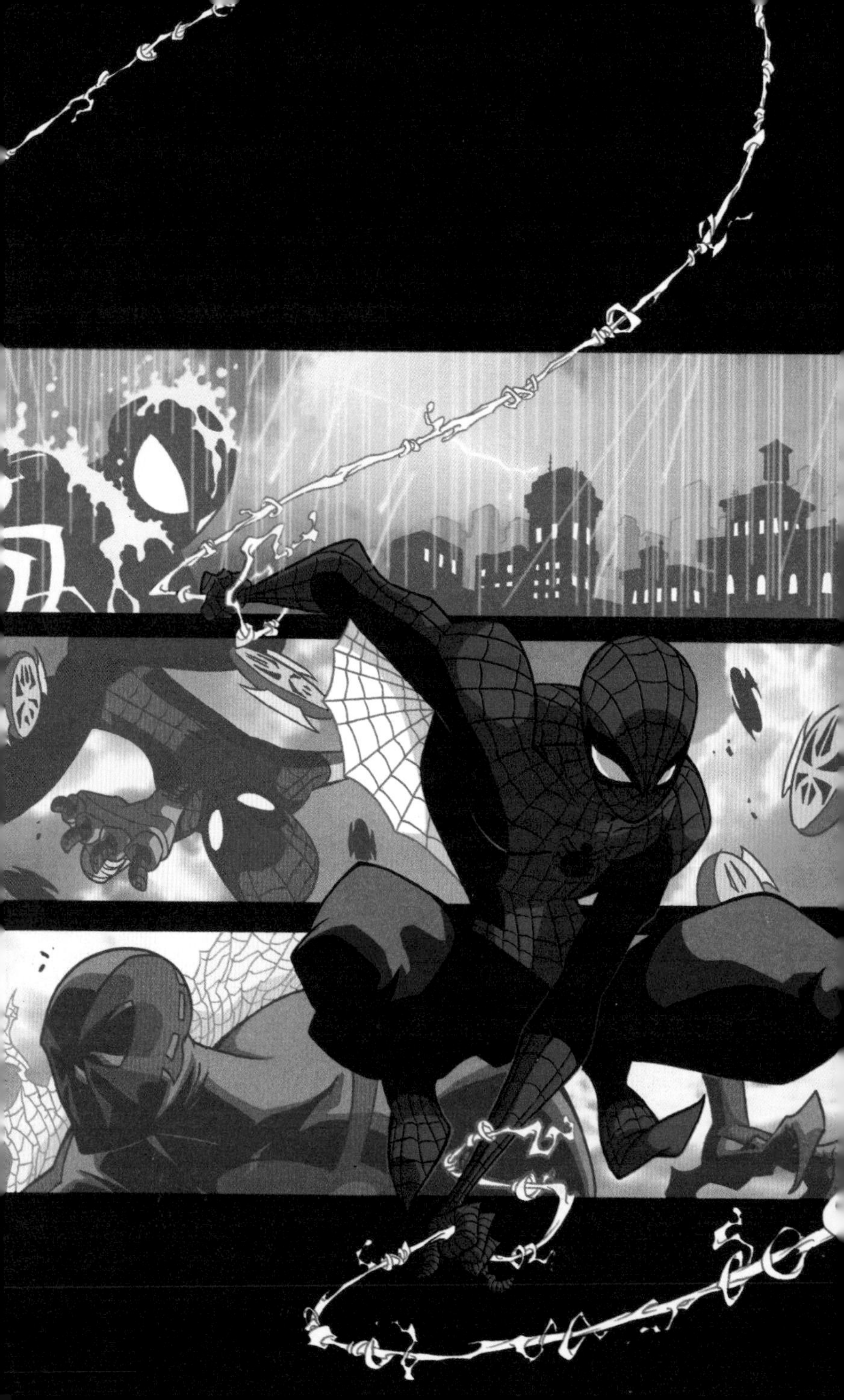

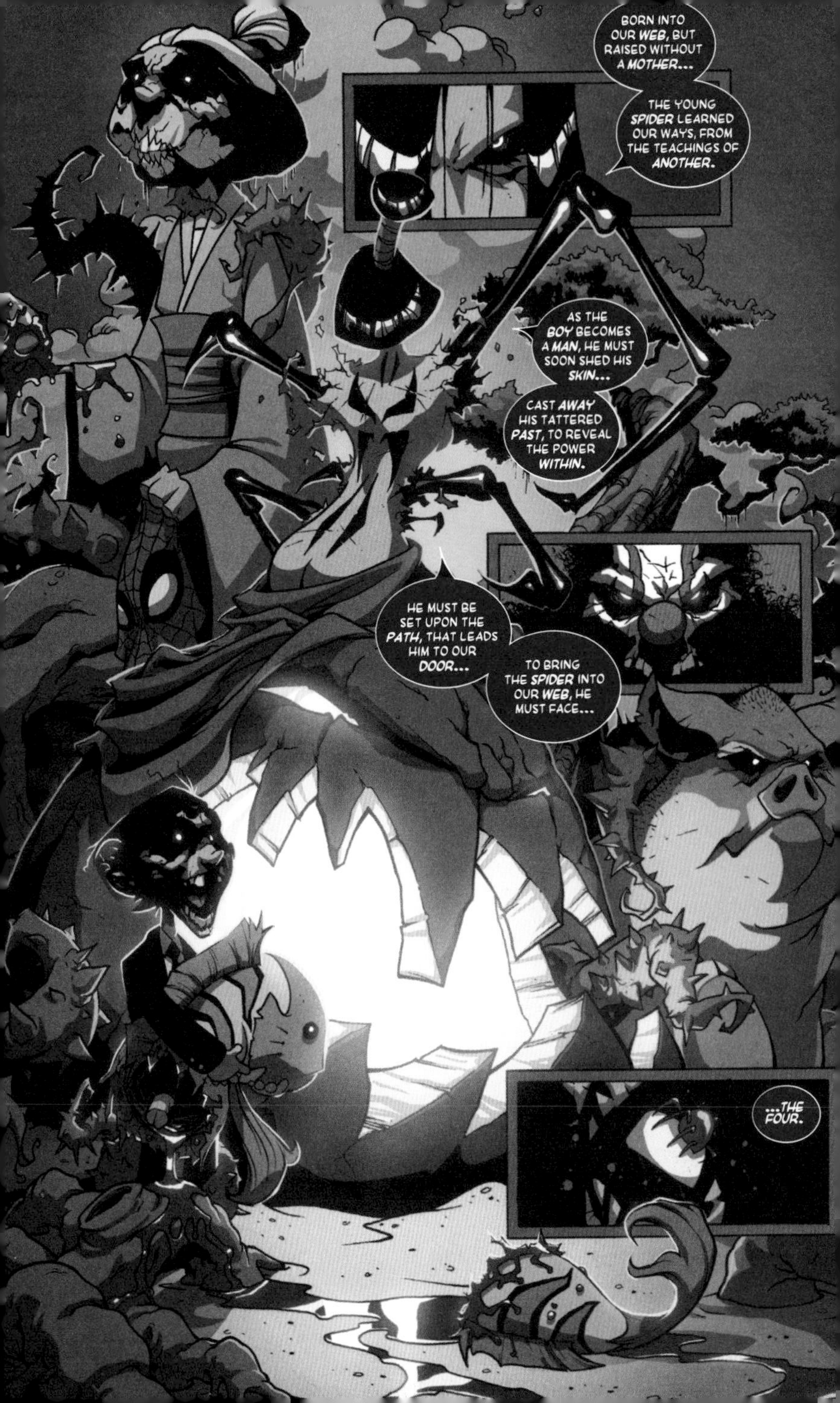
BORN INTO OUR WEB, BUT RAISED WITHOUT A MOTHER...
THE YOUNG SPIDER LEARNED OUR WAYS, FROM THE TEACHINGS OF ANOTHER.
AS THE BOY BECOMES A MAN, HE MUST SOON SHED HIS SKIN...
CAST AWAY HIS TATTERED PAST, TO REVEAL THE POWER WITHIN.
HE MUST BE SET UPON THE PATH, THAT LEADS HIM TO OUR DOOR...
TO BRING THE SPIDER INTO OUR WEB, HE MUST FACE...
...THE FOUR.

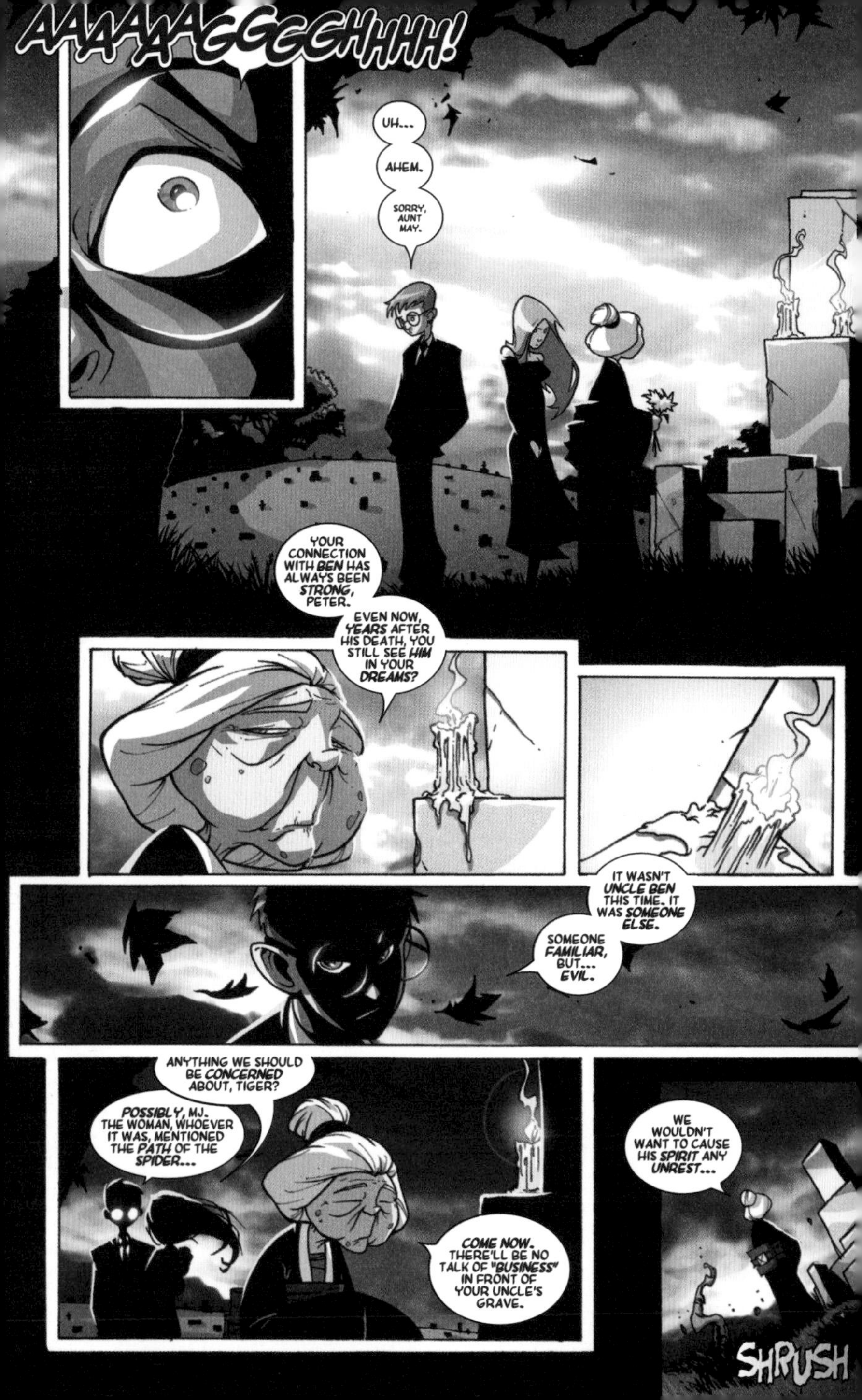
AAAAAAGGGGHHHH!
UH...
AHEM.
SORRY, AUNT MAY.
YOUR CONNECTION WITH BEN HAS ALWAYS BEEN STRONG, PETER.
EVEN NOW, YEARS AFTER HIS DEATH, YOU STILL SEE HIM IN YOUR DREAMS?
IT WASN'T UNCLE BEN THIS TIME. IT WAS SOMEONE ELSE.
SOMEONE FAMILIAR, BUT... EVIL.
ANYTHING WE SHOULD BE CONCERNED ABOUT, TIGER?
POSSIBLY, MJ. THE WOMAN, WHOEVER IT WAS, MENTIONED THE PATH OF THE SPIDER...
COME NOW. THERE'LL BE NO TALK OF "BUSINESS" IN FRONT OF YOUR UNCLE'S GRAVE.
WE WOULDN'T WANT TO CAUSE HIS SPIRIT ANY UNREST...
SHRUSH

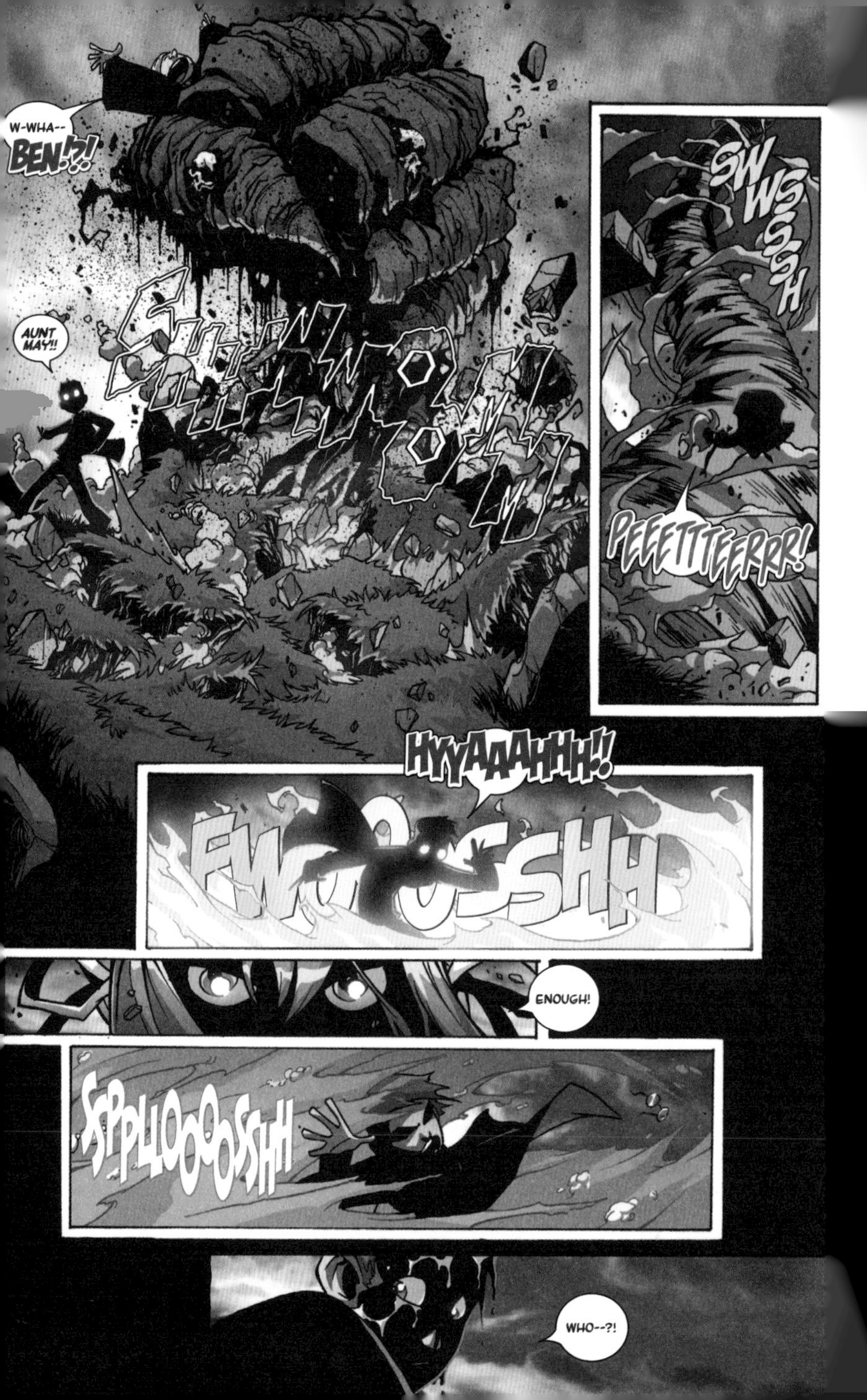
W-WHA--
BEN!?!
AUNT MAY!!
SWWSSH
PEEETTTEERRR!
HYYAAAHHH!!
FWOOSSHH
ENOUGH!
SSPPLLOOOOSSHH
WHO--?!

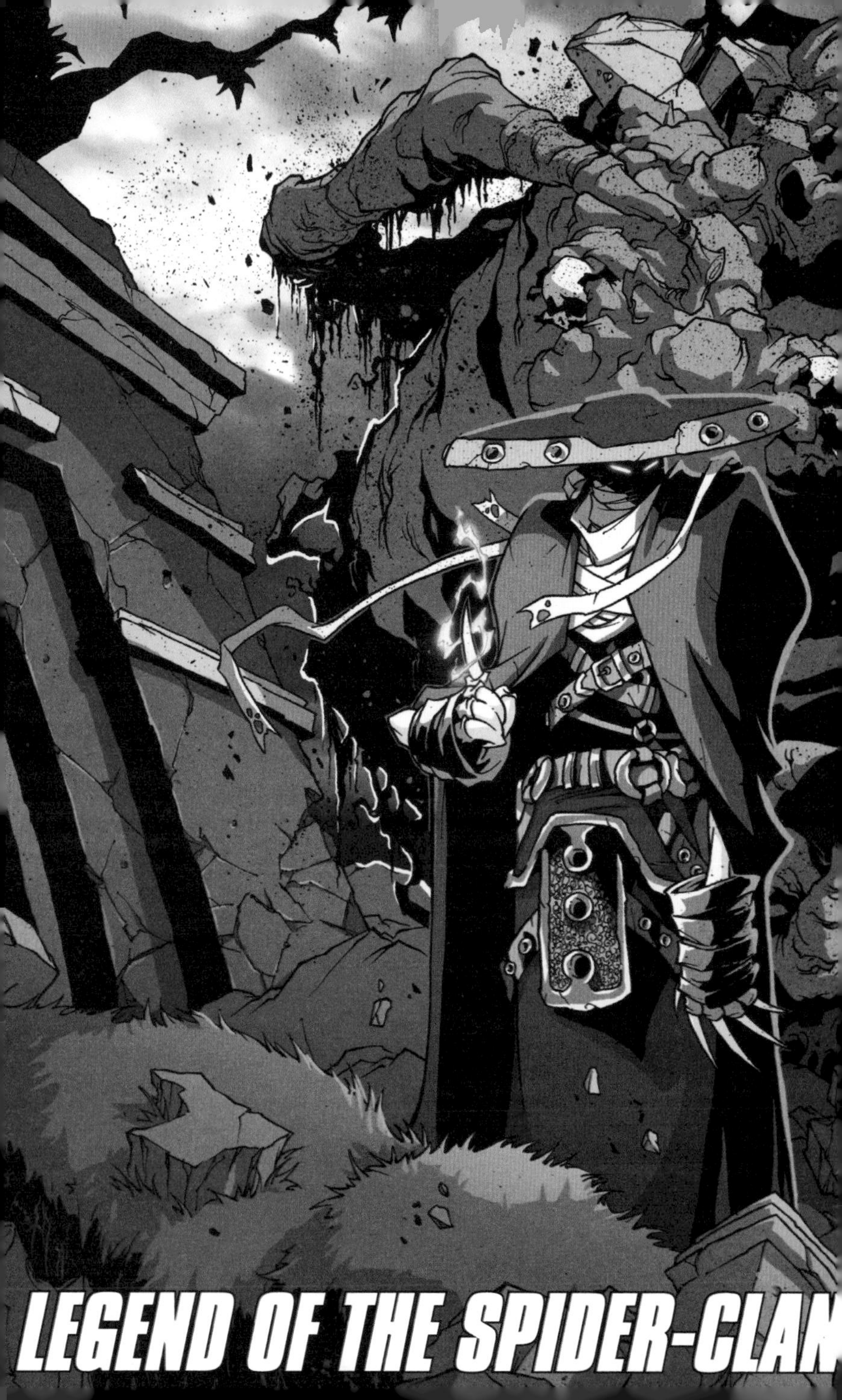
LEGEND OF THE SPIDER-CLAN

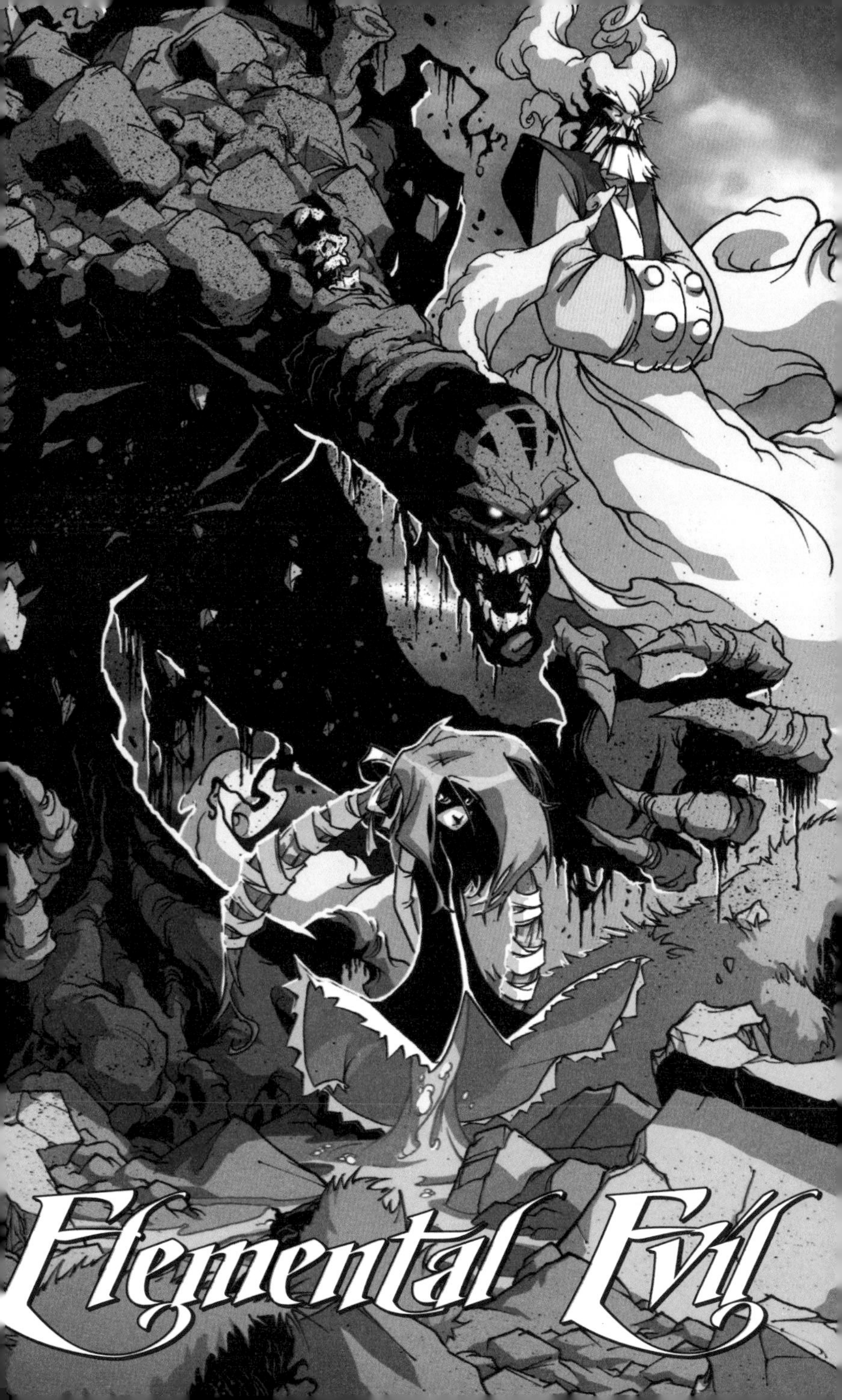
Elemental Evil

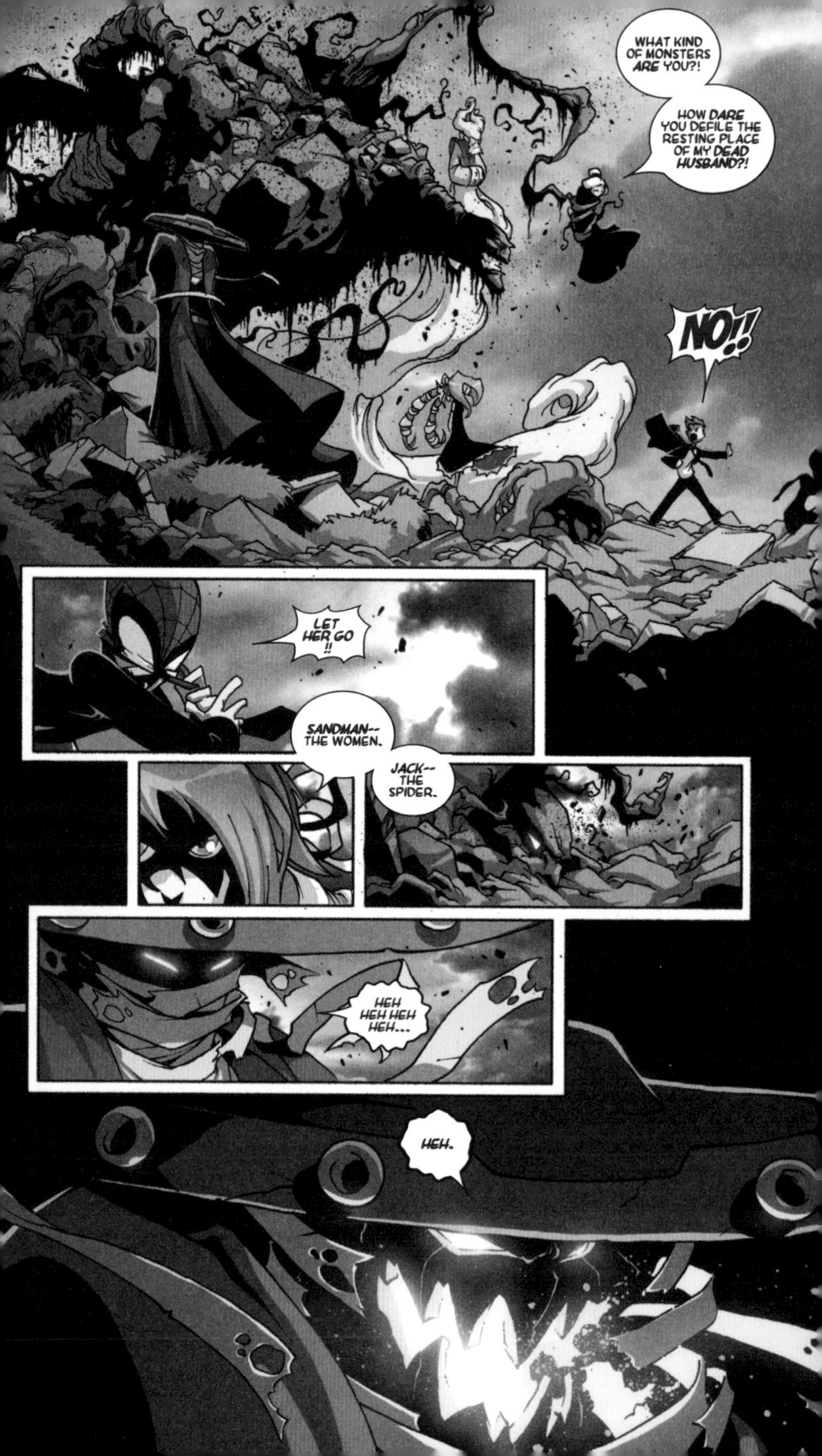

WHAT KIND OF MONSTERS ARE YOU?!
HOW DARE YOU DEFILE THE RESTING PLACE OF MY DEAD HUSBAND?!
NO!!
LET HER GO !!
SANDMAN-- THE WOMEN.
JACK-- THE SPIDER.
HEH HEH HEH HEH...
HEH.

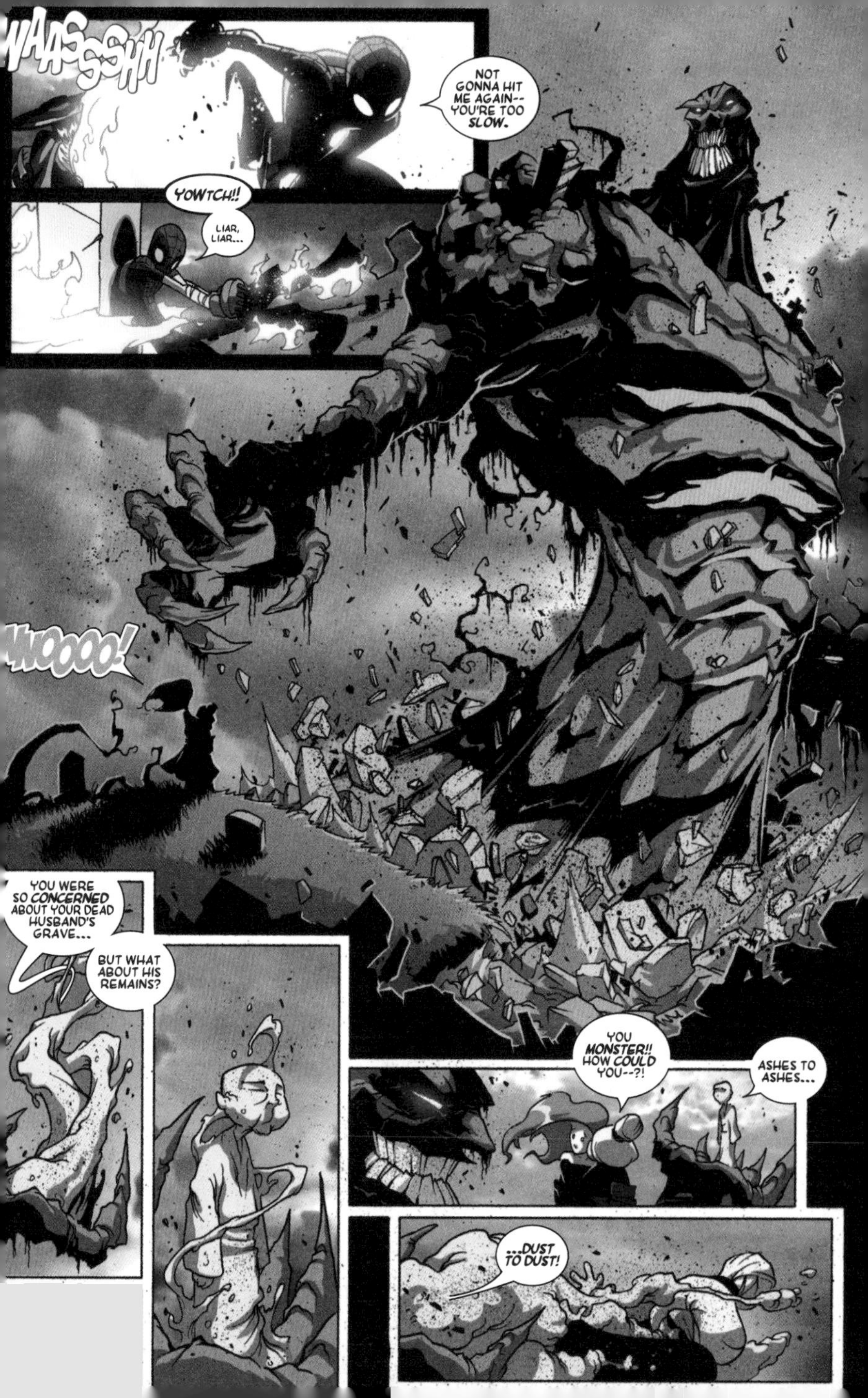
WAASSSHH
NOT GONNA HIT ME AGAIN-- YOU'RE TOO SLOW.
YOWTCH!!
LIAR, LIAR...
WOOOO!
YOU WERE SO CONCERNED ABOUT YOUR DEAD HUSBAND'S GRAVE...
BUT WHAT ABOUT HIS REMAINS?
YOU MONSTER!! HOW COULD YOU--?!
ASHES TO ASHES...
...DUST TO DUST!

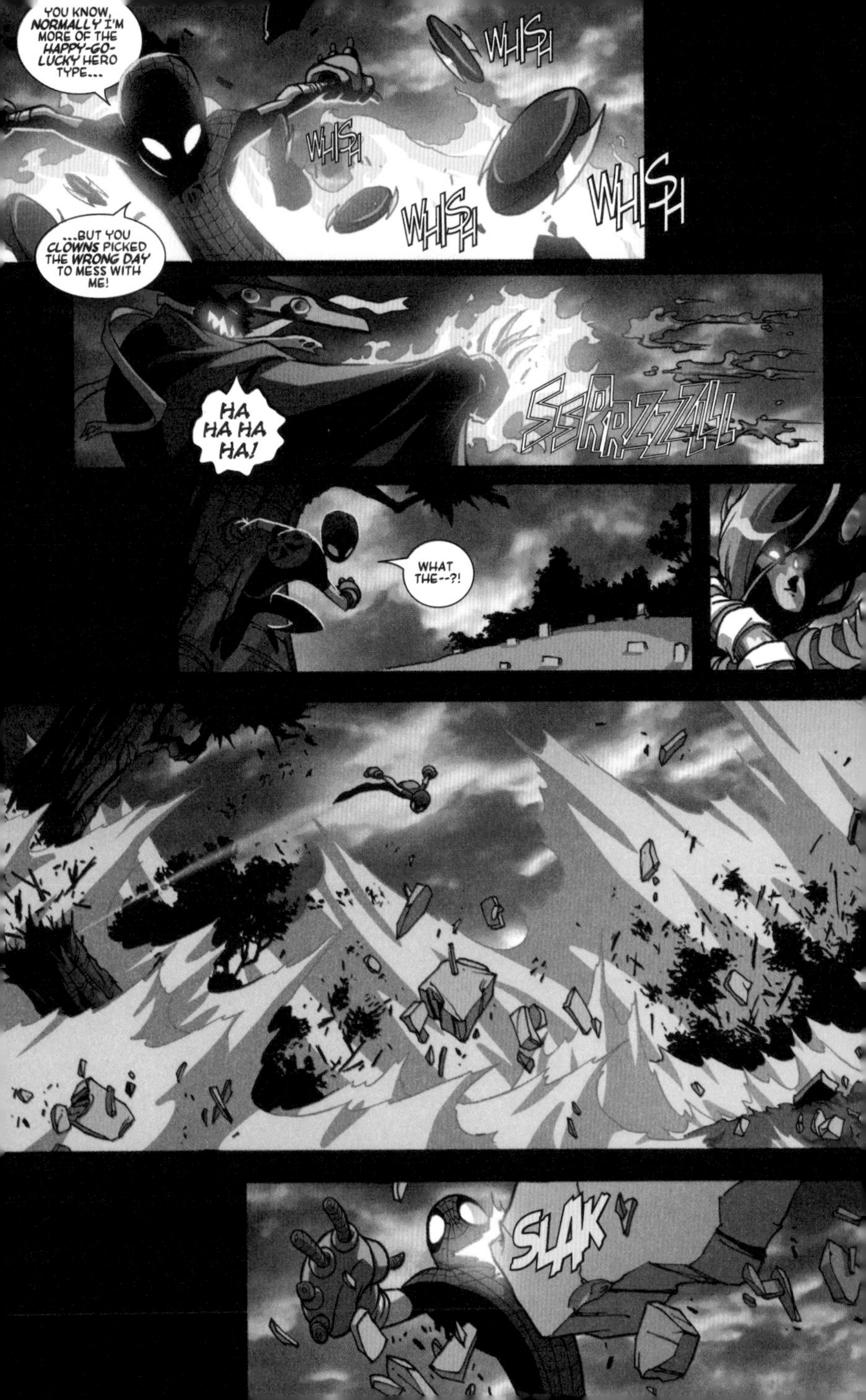
YOU KNOW, NORMALLY I'M MORE OF THE HAPPY-GO-LUCKY HERO TYPE...
WHISH
WHISH
WHISH
WHISH
...BUT YOU CLOWNS PICKED THE WRONG DAY TO MESS WITH ME!
HA HA HA HA!
SSRRZZZLL
WHAT THE--?!
SLAK

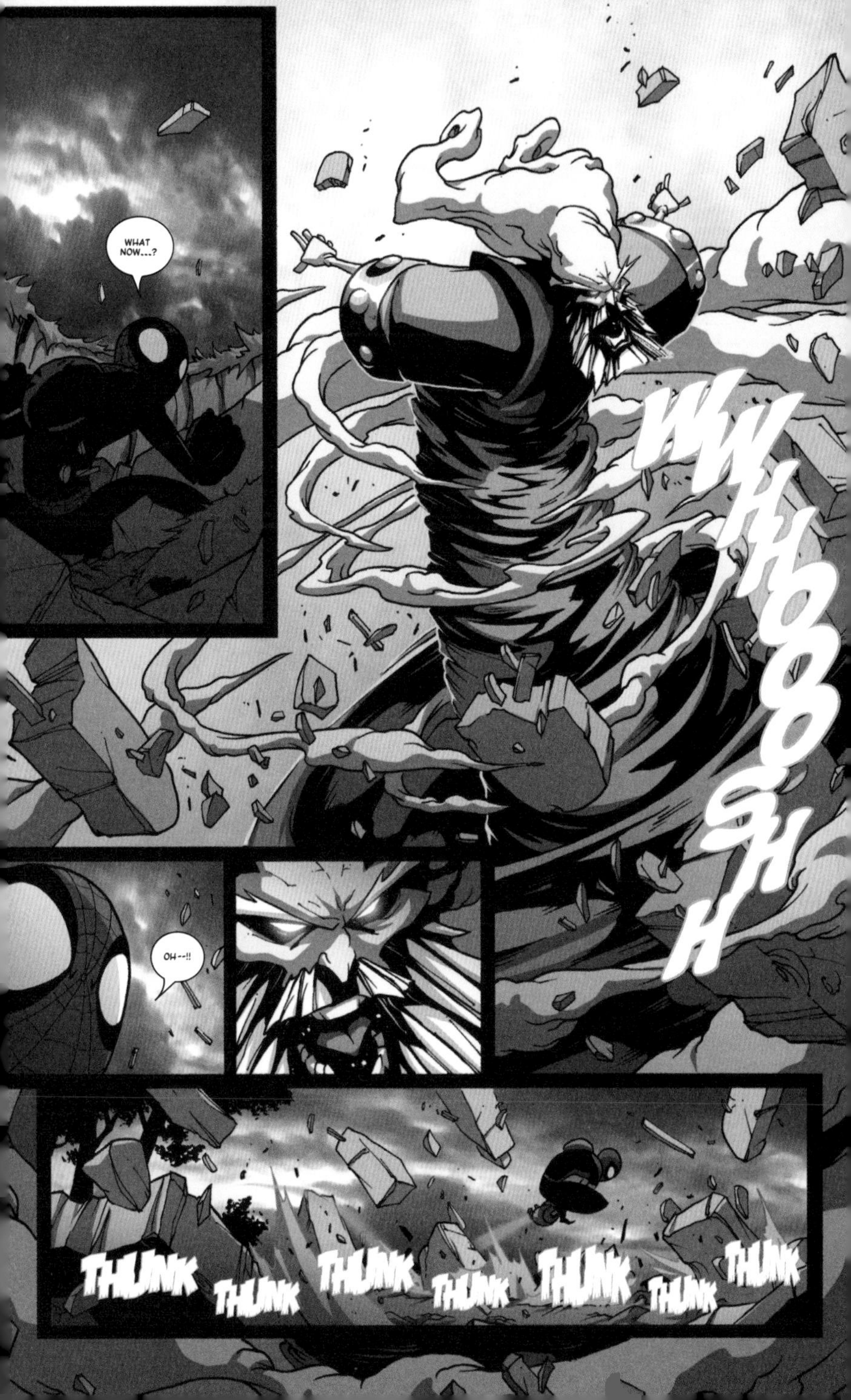
WHAT NOW...?
WHHOOOOSHH
OH--!!
THUNK THUNK THUNK THUNK THUNK THUNK THUNK

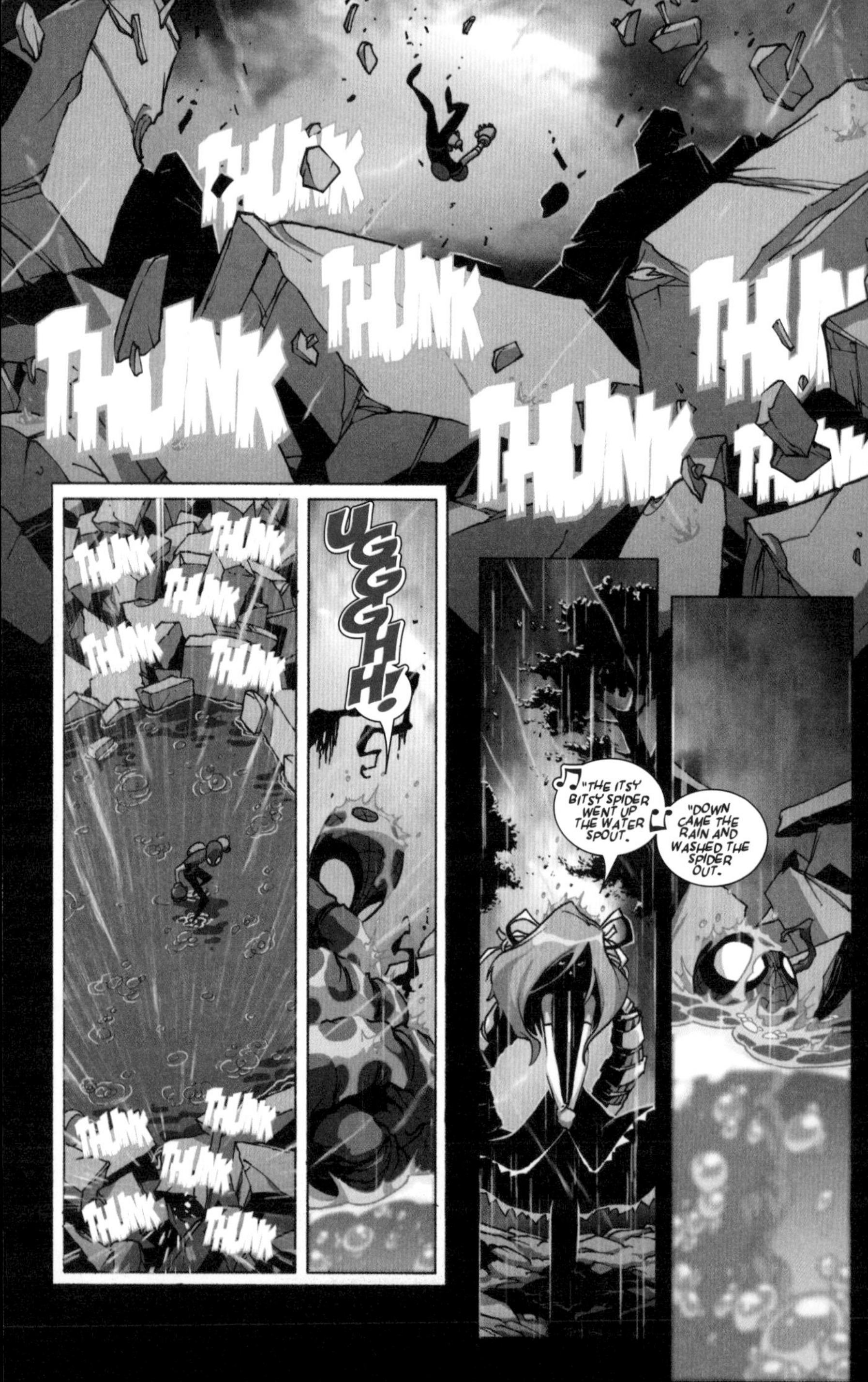
THUNK
THUNK
THUNK
THUNK
THUNK
THUNK
THUNK
THUNK
THUNK
THUNK
THUNK
UGGGH!
THUNK
THUNK
THUNK
THUNK
"THE ITSY BITSY SPIDER WENT UP THE WATER SPOUT.
"DOWN CAME THE RAIN AND WASHED THE SPIDER OUT.

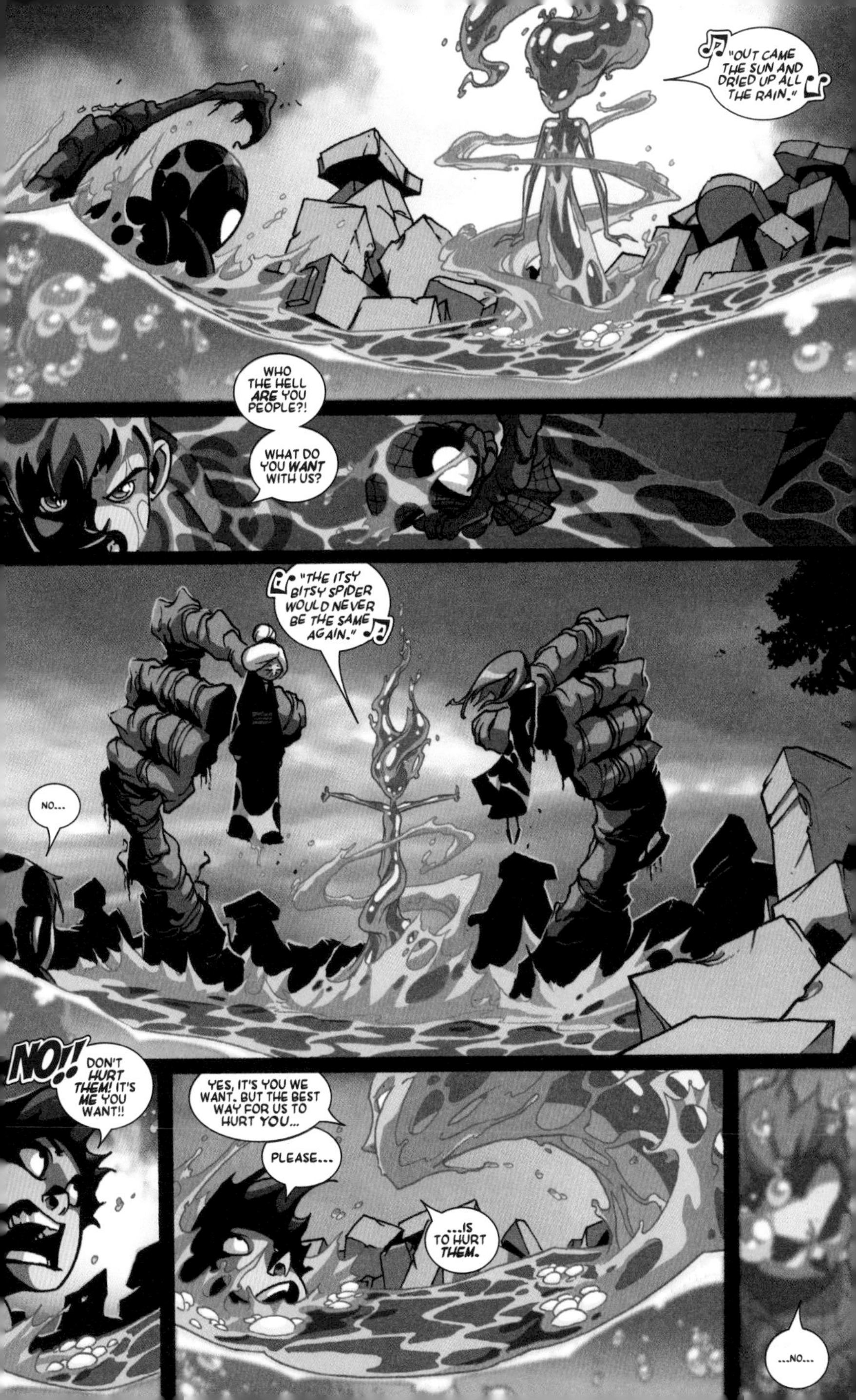
"OUT CAME THE SUN AND DRIED UP ALL THE RAIN."
WHO THE HELL ARE YOU PEOPLE?!
WHAT DO YOU WANT WITH US?
"THE ITSY BITSY SPIDER WOULD NEVER BE THE SAME AGAIN."
NO...
NO!!
DON'T HURT THEM! IT'S ME YOU WANT!!
YES, IT'S YOU WE WANT. BUT THE BEST WAY FOR US TO HURT YOU...
PLEASE...
...IS TO HURT THEM.
...NO...

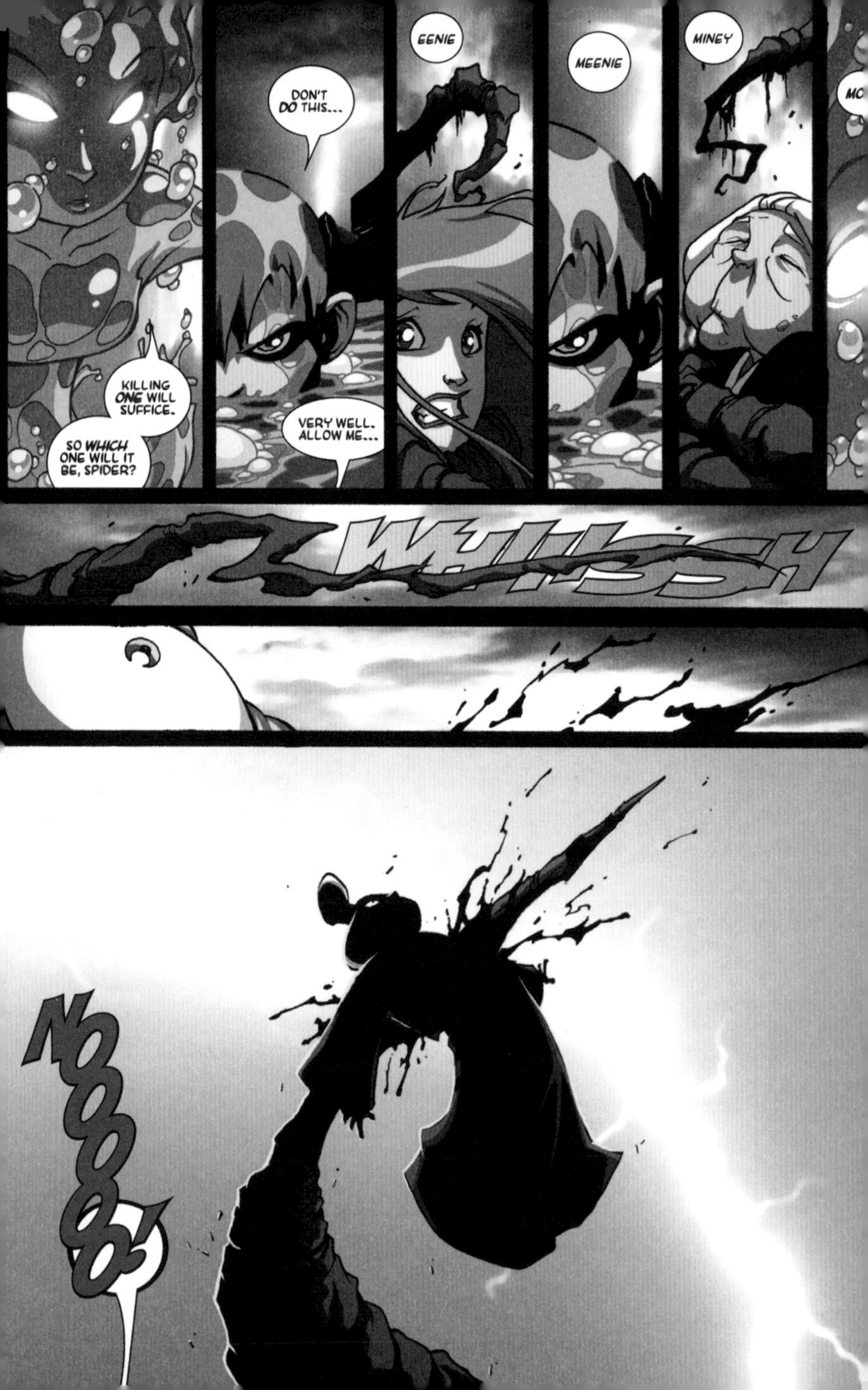
KILLING ONE WILL SUFFICE.
SO WHICH ONE WILL IT BE, SPIDER?
DON'T DO THIS...
VERY WELL. ALLOW ME...
EENIE
MEENIE
MINEY
WHHSSH
NOOOOO

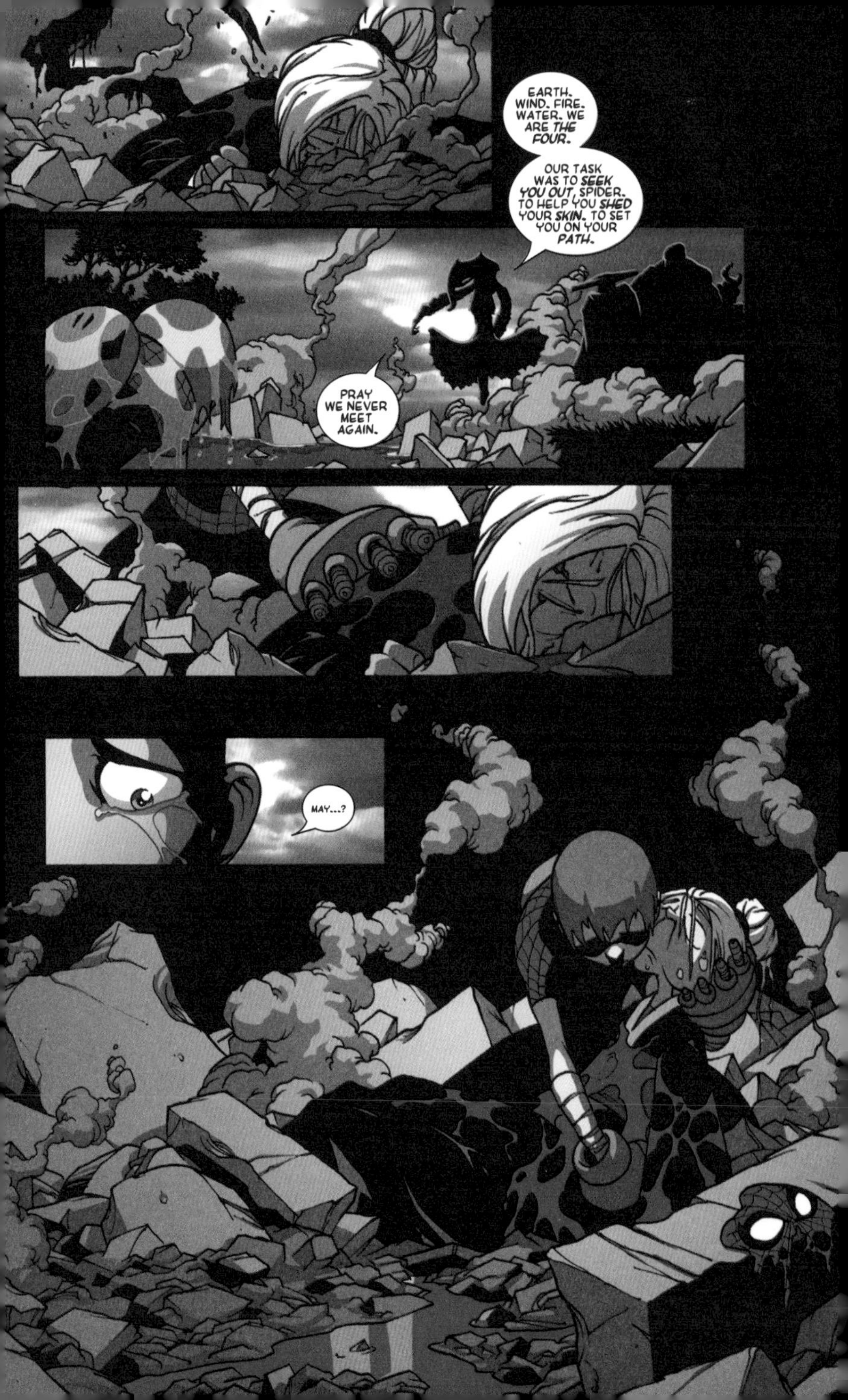

EARTH. WIND. FIRE. WATER. WE ARE THE FOUR.
OUR TASK WAS TO SEEK YOU OUT, SPIDER. TO HELP YOU SHED YOUR SKIN. TO SET YOU ON YOUR PATH.
PRAY WE NEVER MEET AGAIN.
MAY...?

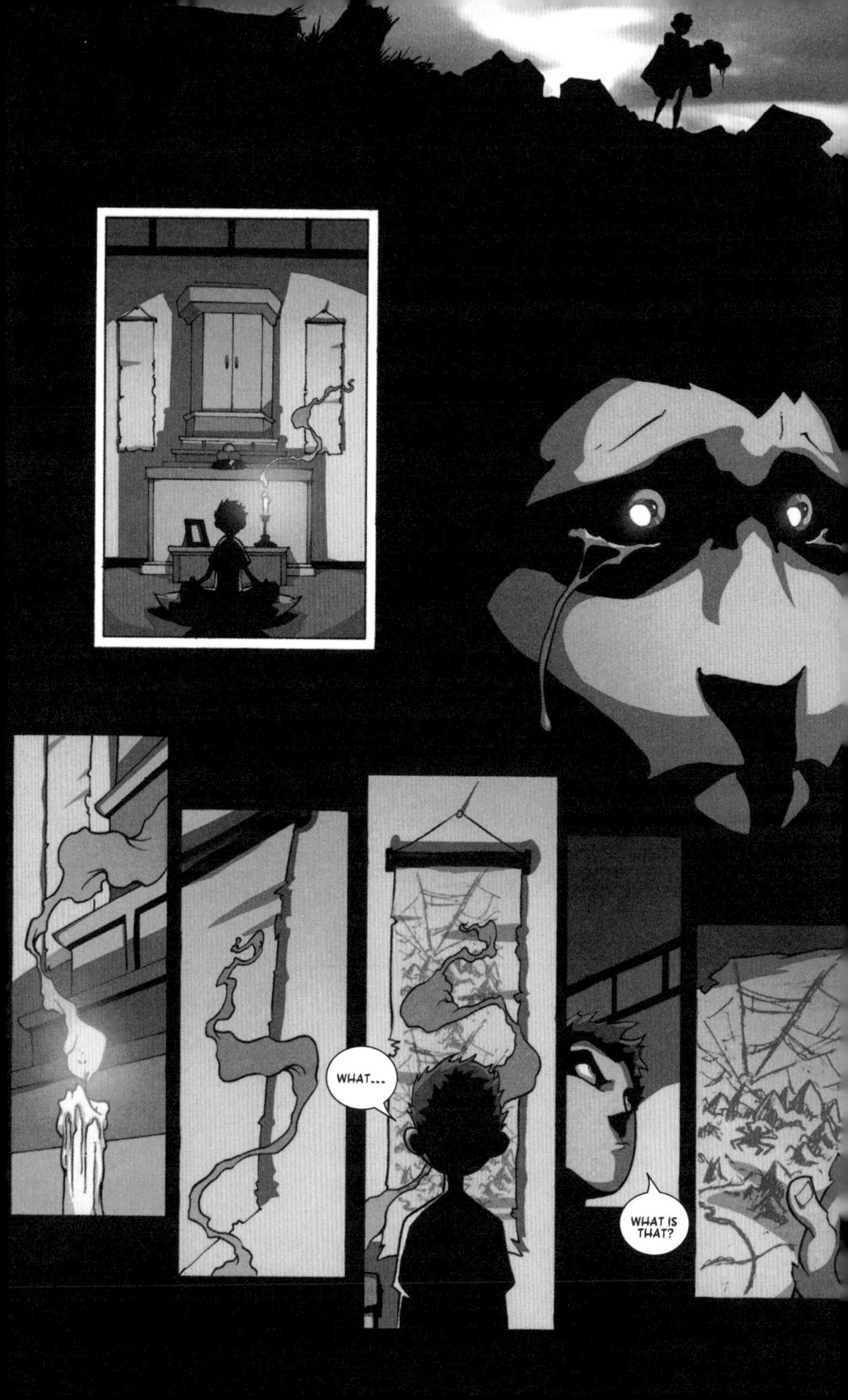
WHAT...
WHAT IS THAT?

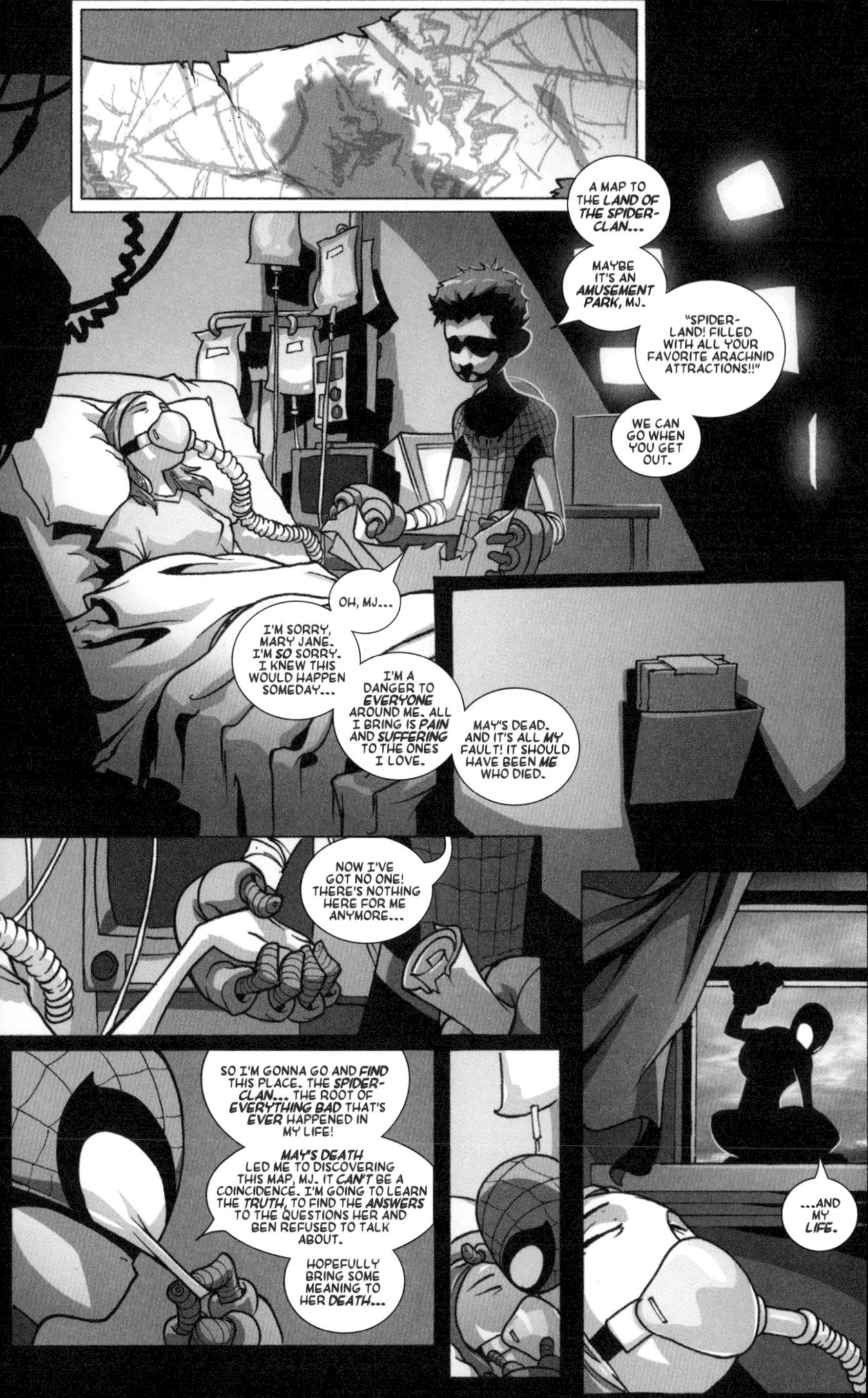
A MAP TO THE LAND OF THE SPIDER-CLAN...
MAYBE IT'S AN AMUSEMENT PARK, MJ.
"SPIDER-LAND! FILLED WITH ALL YOUR FAVORITE ARACHNID ATTRACTIONS!!"
WE CAN GO WHEN YOU GET OUT.
OH, MJ...
I'M SORRY, MARY JANE. I'M SO SORRY. I KNEW THIS WOULD HAPPEN SOMEDAY...
I'M A DANGER TO EVERYONE AROUND ME. ALL I BRING IS PAIN AND SUFFERING TO THE ONES I LOVE.
MAY'S DEAD. AND IT'S ALL MY FAULT! IT SHOULD HAVE BEEN ME WHO DIED.
NOW I'VE GOT NO ONE! THERE'S NOTHING HERE FOR ME ANYMORE...
SO I'M GONNA GO AND FIND THIS PLACE. THE SPIDER-CLAN... THE ROOT OF EVERYTHING BAD THAT'S EVER HAPPENED IN MY LIFE!
MAY'S DEATH LED ME TO DISCOVERING THIS MAP, MJ. IT CAN'T BE A COINCIDENCE. I'M GOING TO LEARN THE TRUTH, TO FIND THE ANSWERS TO THE QUESTIONS HER AND BEN REFUSED TO TALK ABOUT.
HOPEFULLY BRING SOME MEANING TO HER DEATH...
...AND MY LIFE.

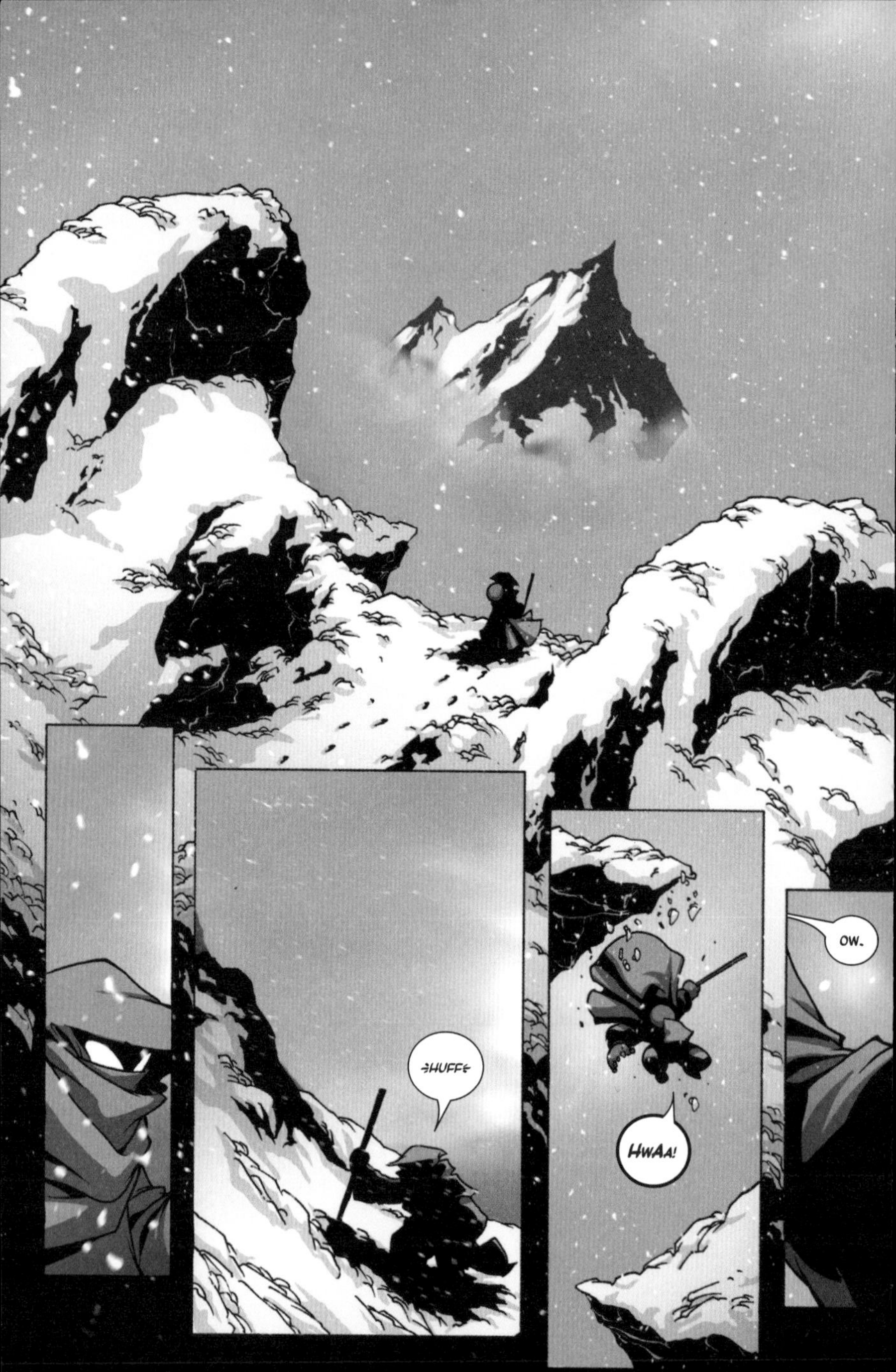

HUFF
HWAA!
OW.

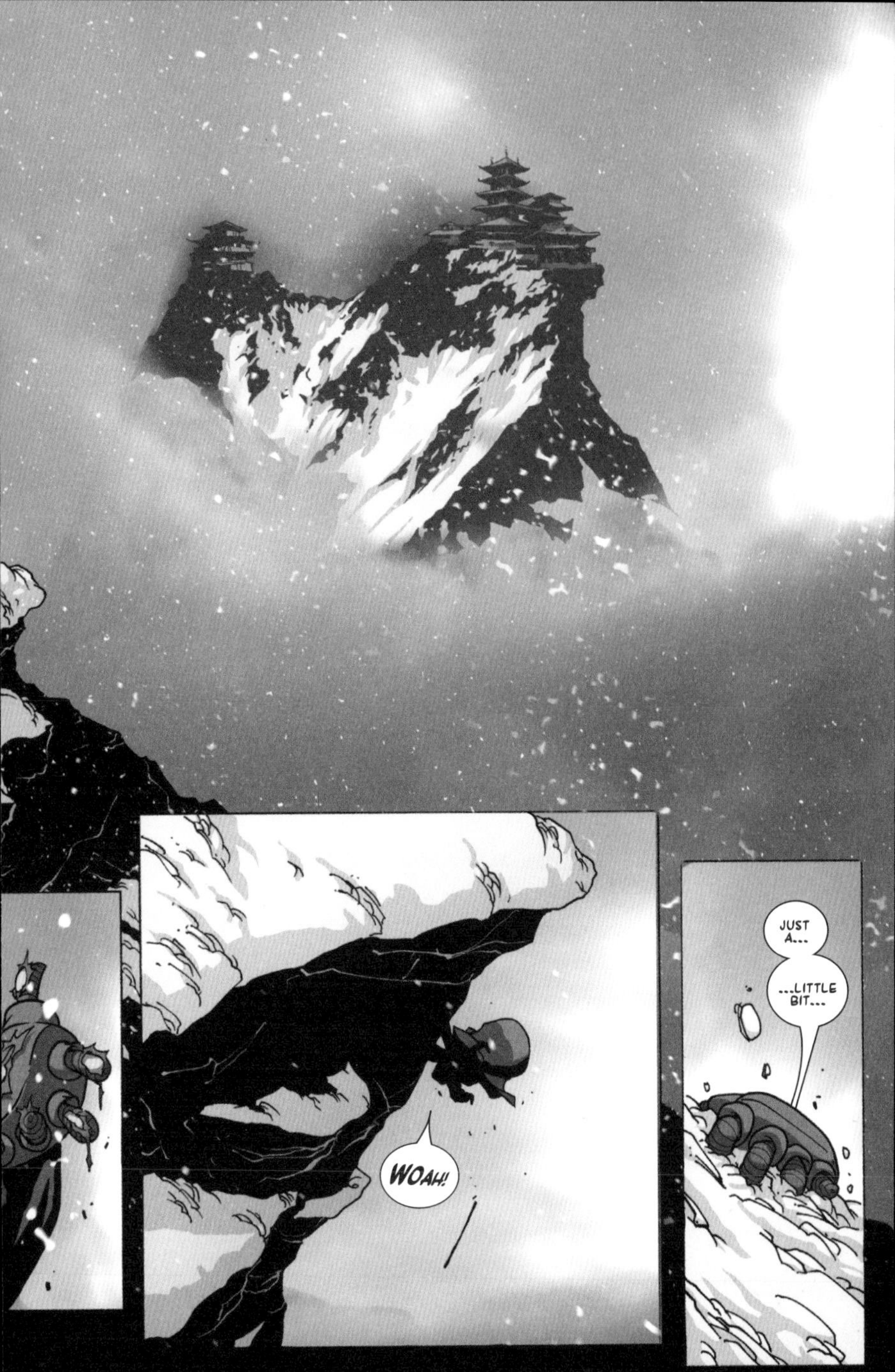
WOAH!
JUST A...
...LITTLE BIT...

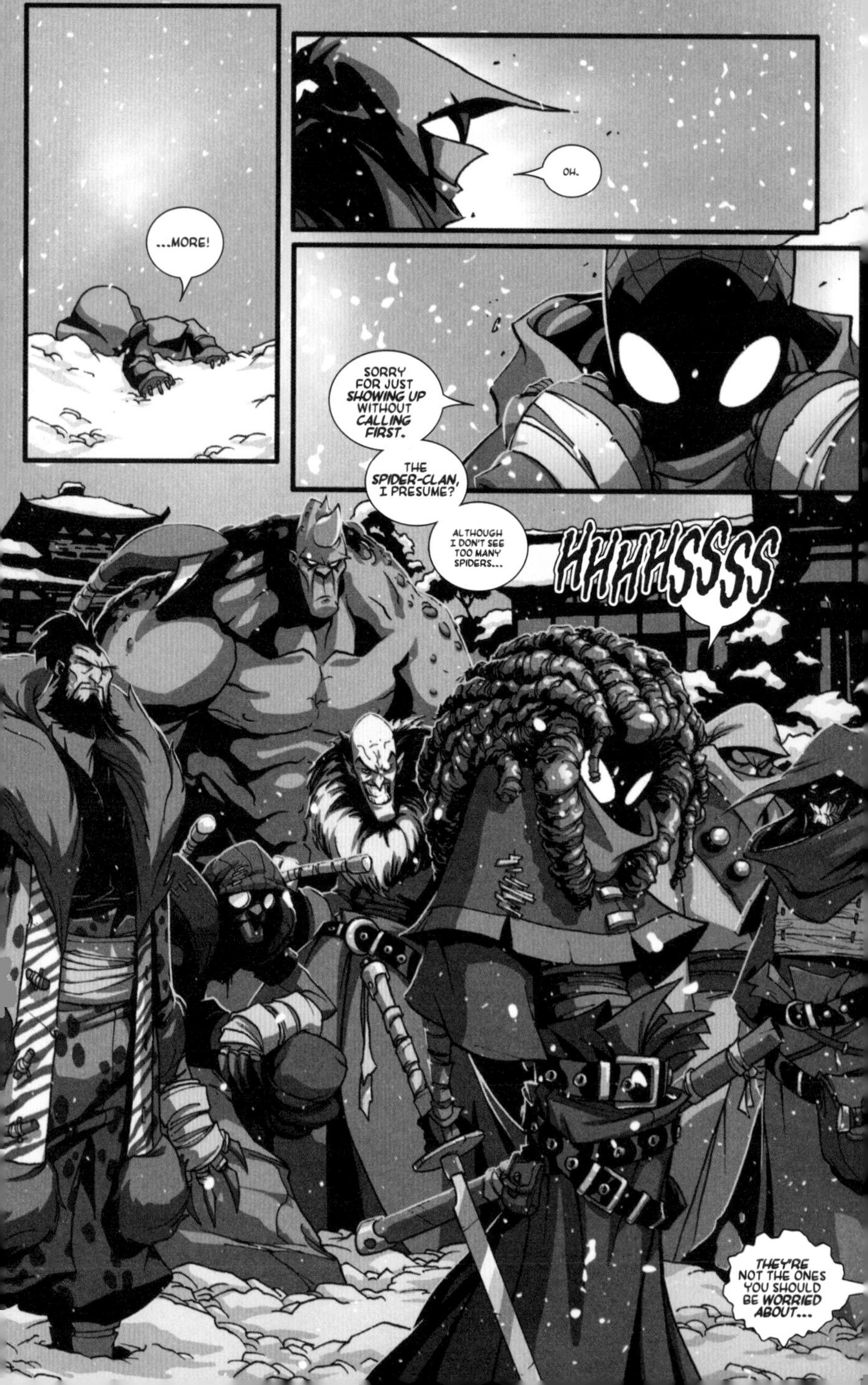
...MORE!
OH.
SORRY FOR JUST SHOWING UP WITHOUT CALLING FIRST.
THE SPIDER-CLAN, I PRESUME?
ALTHOUGH I DON'T SEE TOO MANY SPIDERS...
HHHHSSSSS
THEY'RE NOT THE ONES YOU SHOULD BE WORRIED ABOUT...

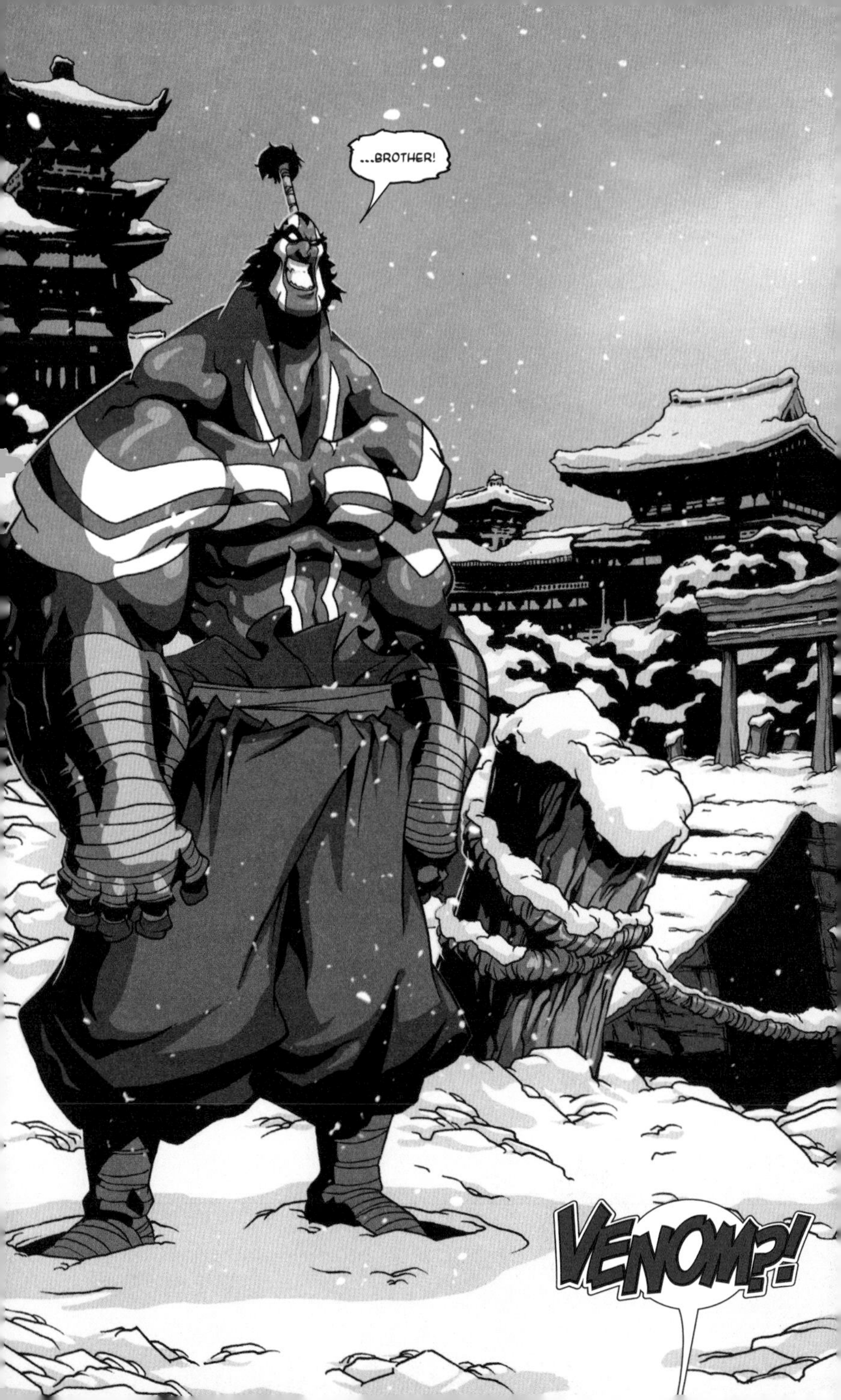
...BROTHER!
VENOM?!

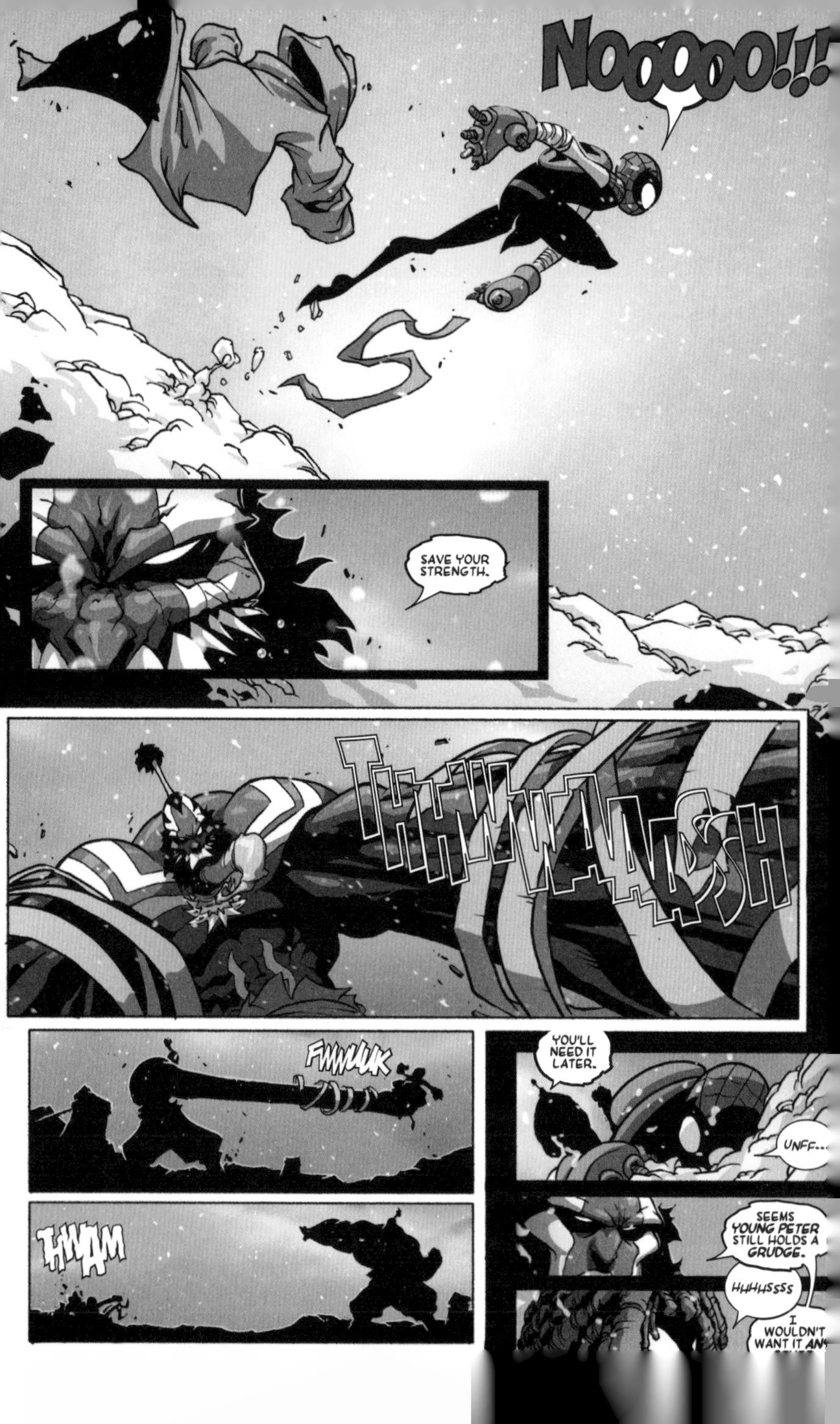
NOOOOO!!!
SAVE YOUR STRENGTH.
THHWWAASH
FWWUUK
THWAM
YOU'LL NEED IT LATER.
UNFF...
SEEMS YOUNG PETER STILL HOLDS A GRUDGE.
HHHHSSSS

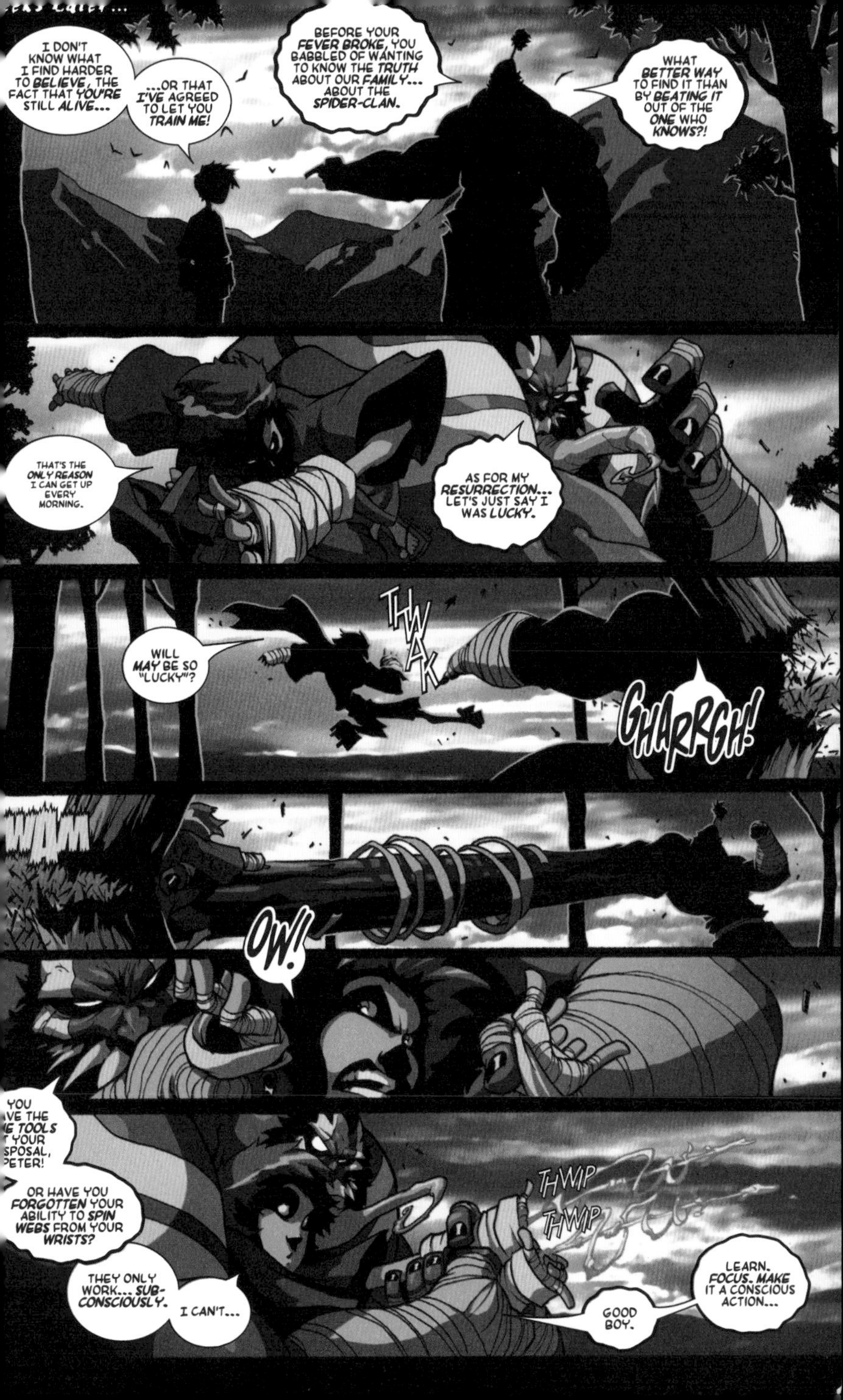
I DON'T KNOW WHAT I FIND HARDER TO BELIEVE, THE FACT THAT YOU'RE STILL ALIVE...
...OR THAT I'VE AGREED TO LET YOU TRAIN ME!
BEFORE YOUR FEVER BROKE, YOU BABBLED OF WANTING TO KNOW THE TRUTH ABOUT OUR FAMILY... ABOUT THE SPIDER-CLAN.
WHAT BETTER WAY TO FIND IT THAN BY BEATING IT OUT OF THE ONE WHO KNOWS?!
THAT'S THE ONLY REASON I CAN GET UP EVERY MORNING.
AS FOR MY RESURRECTION... LET'S JUST SAY I WAS LUCKY.
THWAK
WILL MAY BE SO "LUCKY"?
GHARRGH!
WAM
OW!
OR HAVE YOU FORGOTTEN YOUR ABILITY TO SPIN WEBS FROM YOUR WRISTS?
THWIP
THWIP
THEY ONLY WORK... SUB-CONSCIOUSLY.
I CAN'T...
LEARN. FOCUS. MAKE IT A CONSCIOUS ACTION...
GOOD BOY.

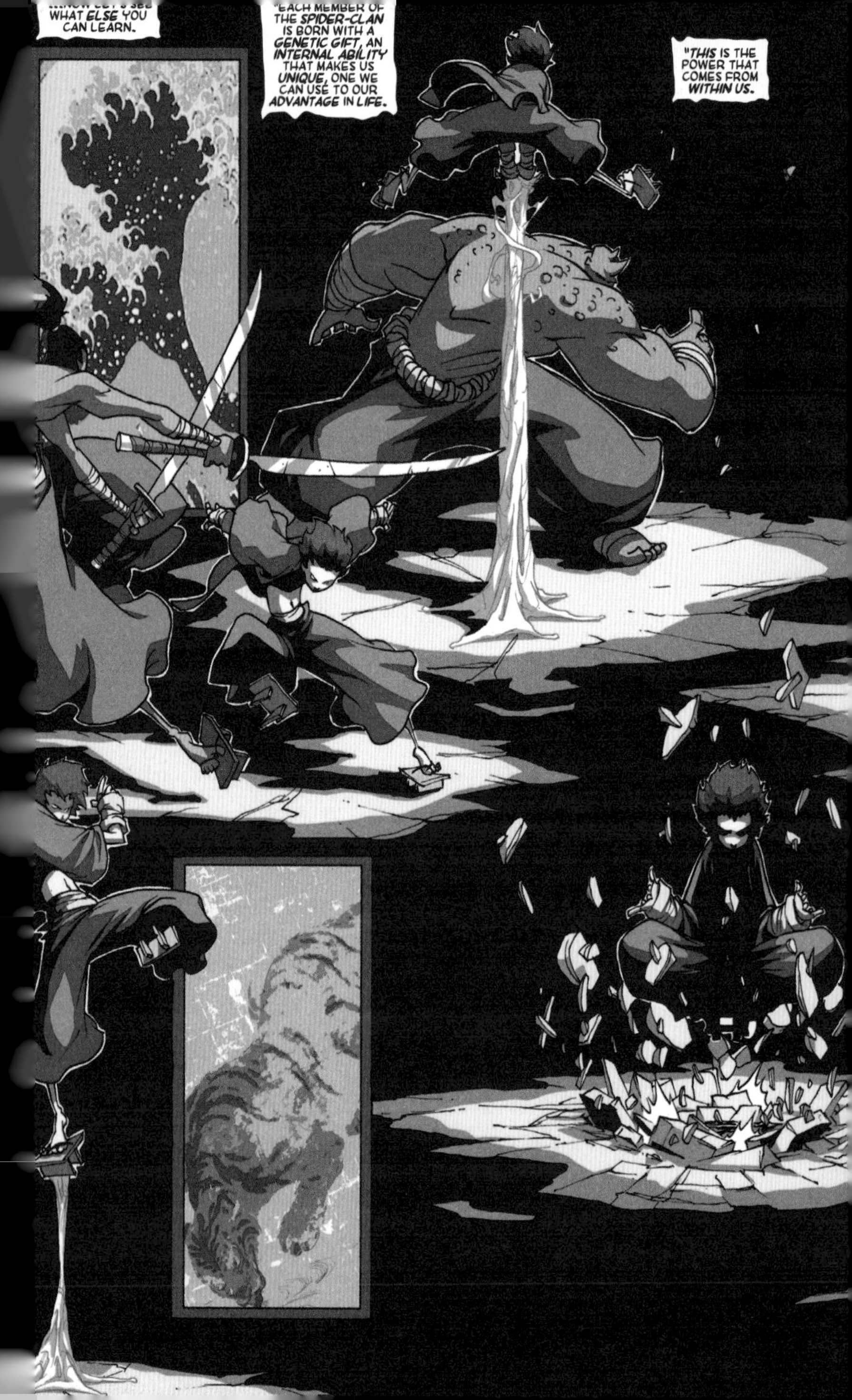
WHAT ELSE YOU CAN LEARN.
"EACH MEMBER OF THE SPIDER-CLAN IS BORN WITH A GENETIC GIFT, AN INTERNAL ABILITY THAT MAKES US UNIQUE, ONE WE CAN USE TO OUR ADVANTAGE IN LIFE.
"THIS IS THE POWER THAT COMES FROM WITHIN US.

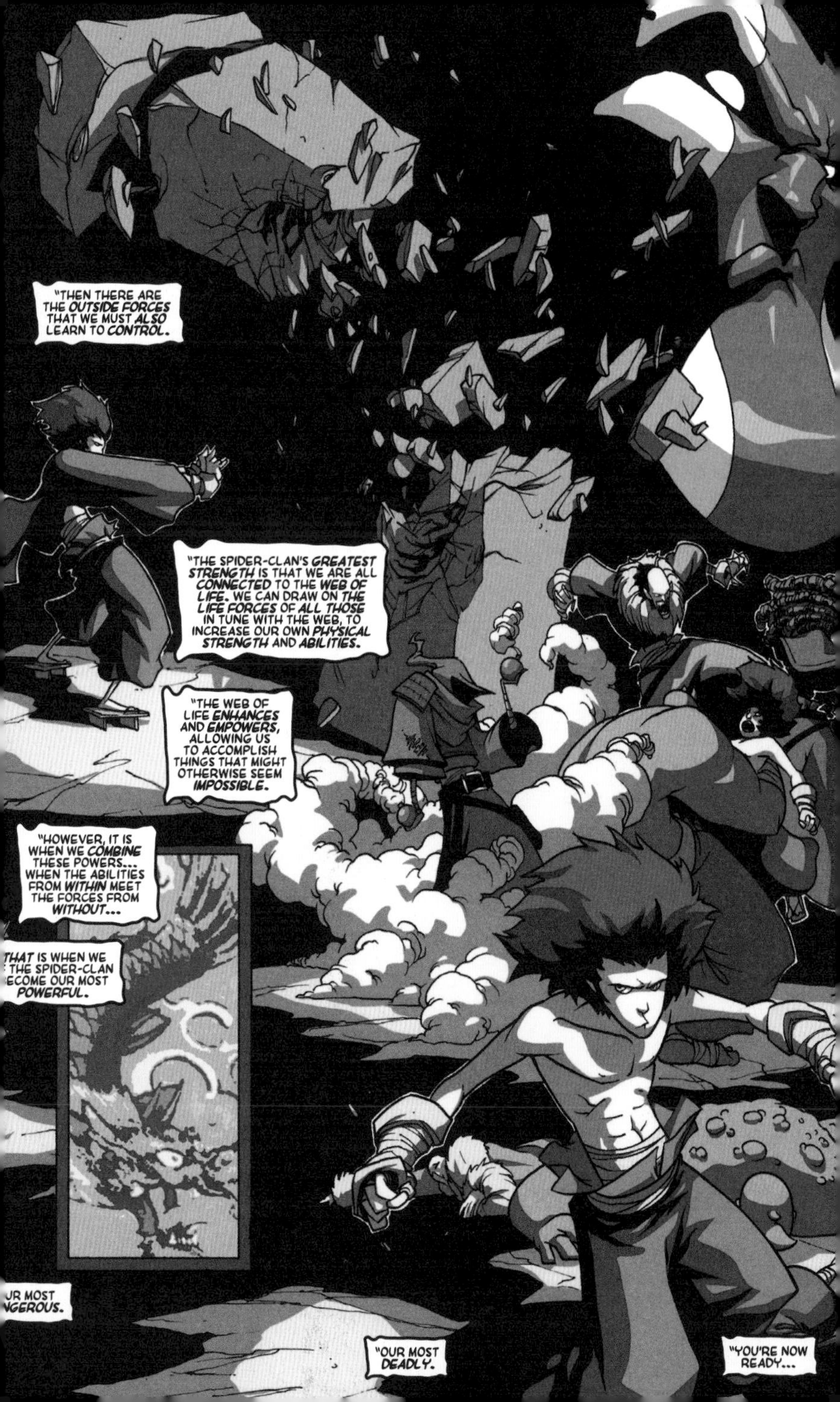
"THEN THERE ARE THE OUTSIDE FORCES THAT WE MUST ALSO LEARN TO CONTROL.
"THE SPIDER-CLAN'S GREATEST STRENGTH IS THAT WE ARE ALL CONNECTED TO THE WEB OF LIFE. WE CAN DRAW ON THE LIFE FORCES OF ALL THOSE IN TUNE WITH THE WEB, TO INCREASE OUR OWN PHYSICAL STRENGTH AND ABILITIES.
"THE WEB OF LIFE ENHANCES AND EMPOWERS, ALLOWING US TO ACCOMPLISH THINGS THAT MIGHT OTHERWISE SEEM IMPOSSIBLE.
"HOWEVER, IT IS WHEN WE COMBINE THESE POWERS... WHEN THE ABILITIES FROM WITHIN MEET THE FORCES FROM WITHOUT...
THAT IS WHEN WE THE SPIDER-CLAN ECOME OUR MOST POWERFUL.
UR MOST NGEROUS.
"OUR MOST DEADLY.
"YOU'RE NOW READY...

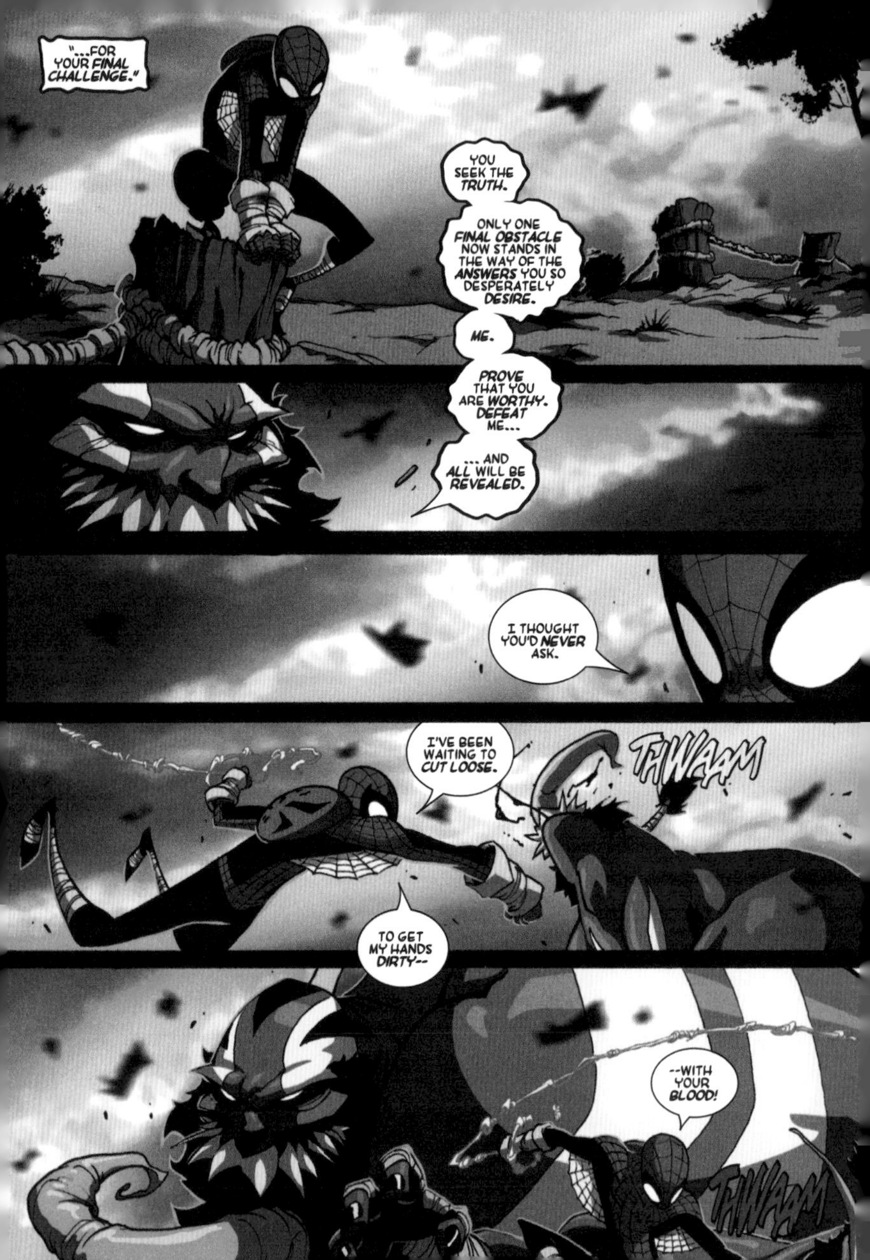
"...FOR YOUR FINAL CHALLENGE."
YOU SEEK THE TRUTH.
ONLY ONE FINAL OBSTACLE NOW STANDS IN THE WAY OF THE ANSWERS YOU SO DESPERATELY DESIRE.
ME.
PROVE THAT YOU ARE WORTHY. DEFEAT ME...
...AND ALL WILL BE REVEALED.
I THOUGHT YOU'D NEVER ASK.
I'VE BEEN WAITING TO CUT LOOSE.
THWAAM
TO GET MY HANDS DIRTY--
--WITH YOUR BLOOD!
THWAAM

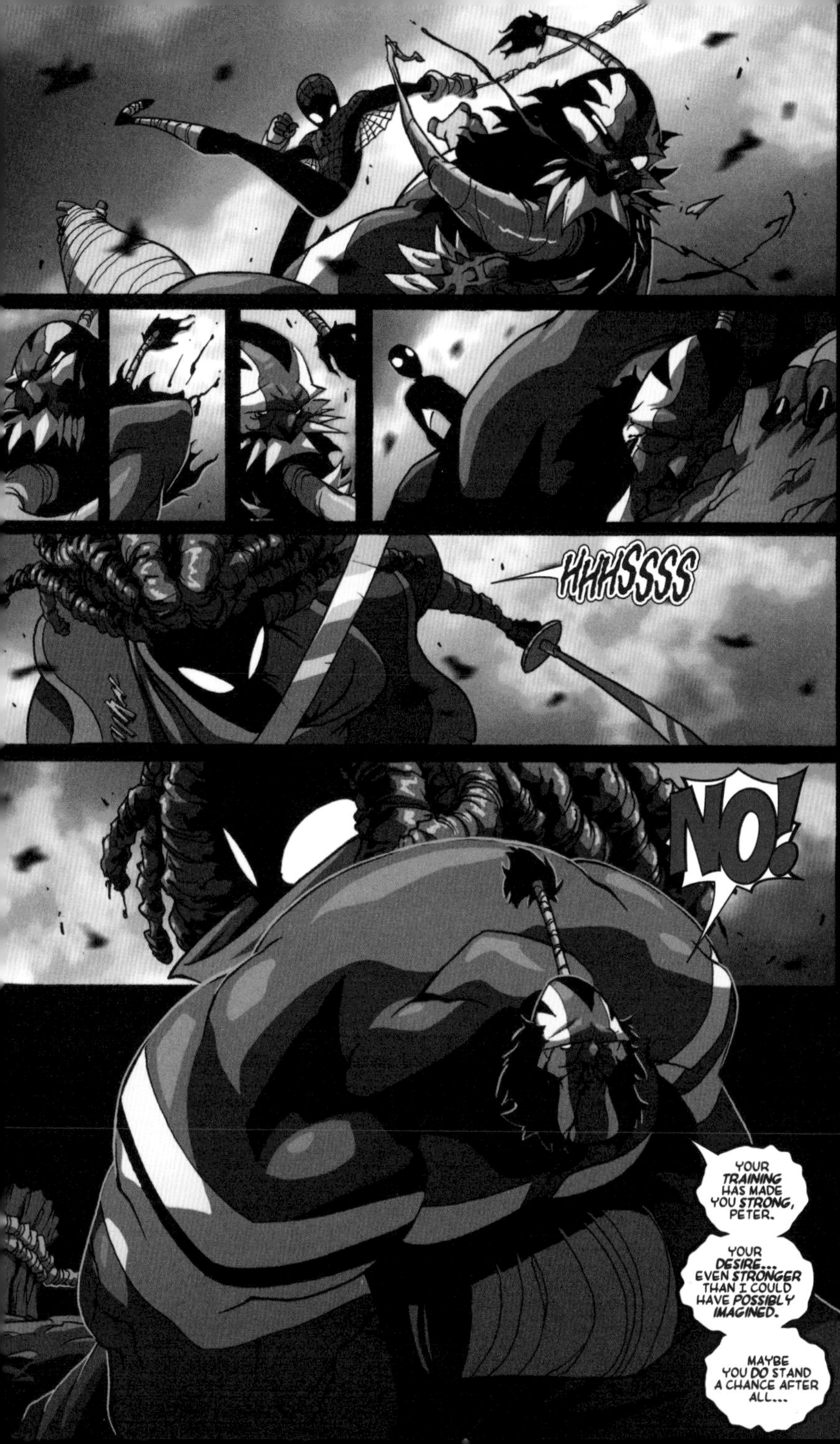
HHHSSSS
NO!
YOUR TRAINING HAS MADE YOU STRONG, PETER.
YOUR DESIRE... EVEN STRONGER THAN I COULD HAVE POSSIBLY IMAGINED.
MAYBE YOU DO STAND A CHANCE AFTER ALL...

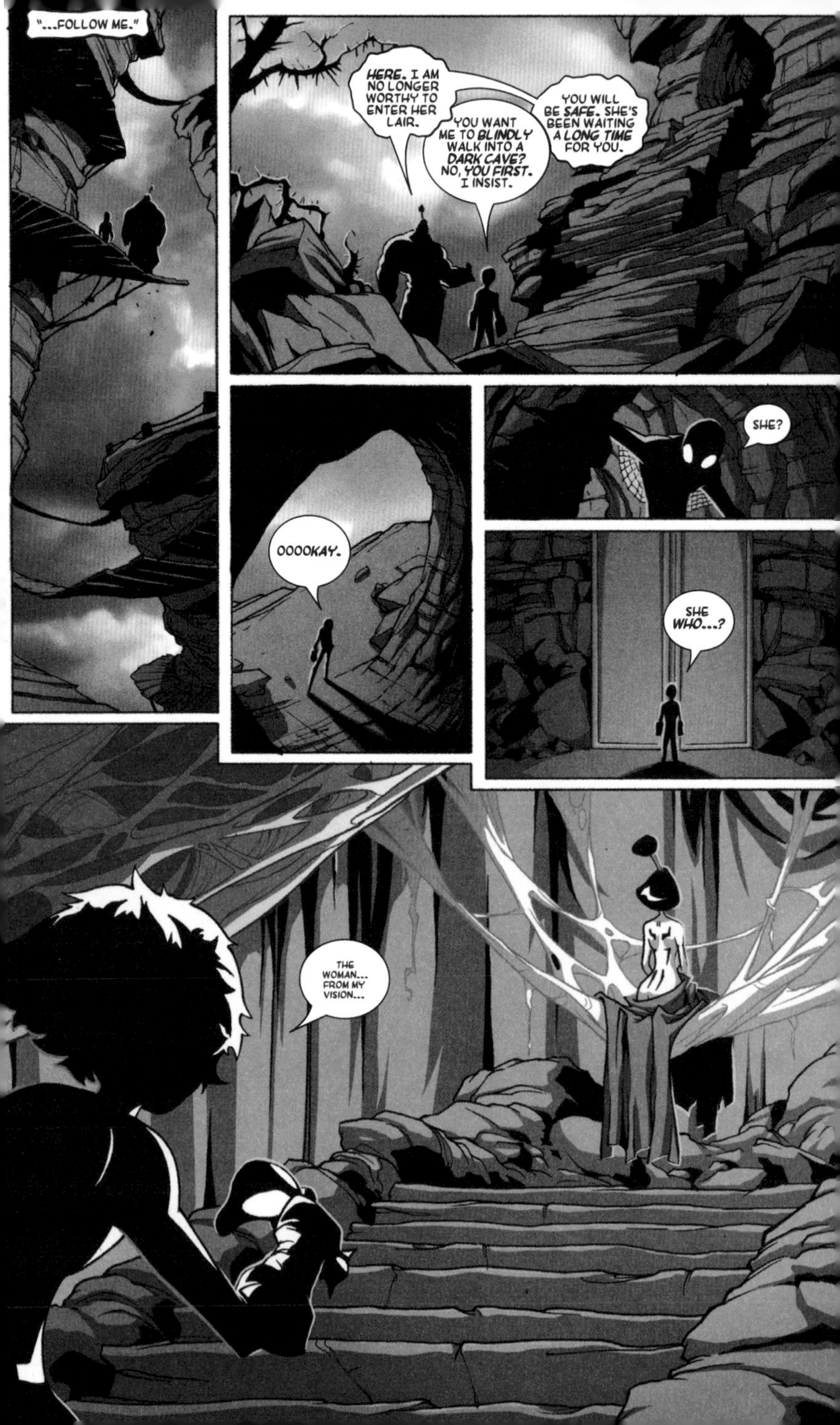
"...FOLLOW ME."
HERE. I AM NO LONGER WORTHY TO ENTER HER LAIR.
YOU WANT ME TO BLINDLY WALK INTO A DARK CAVE? NO, YOU FIRST. I INSIST.
YOU WILL BE SAFE. SHE'S BEEN WAITING A LONG TIME FOR YOU.
OOOOKAY.
SHE?
SHE WHO...?
THE WOMAN... FROM MY VISION...

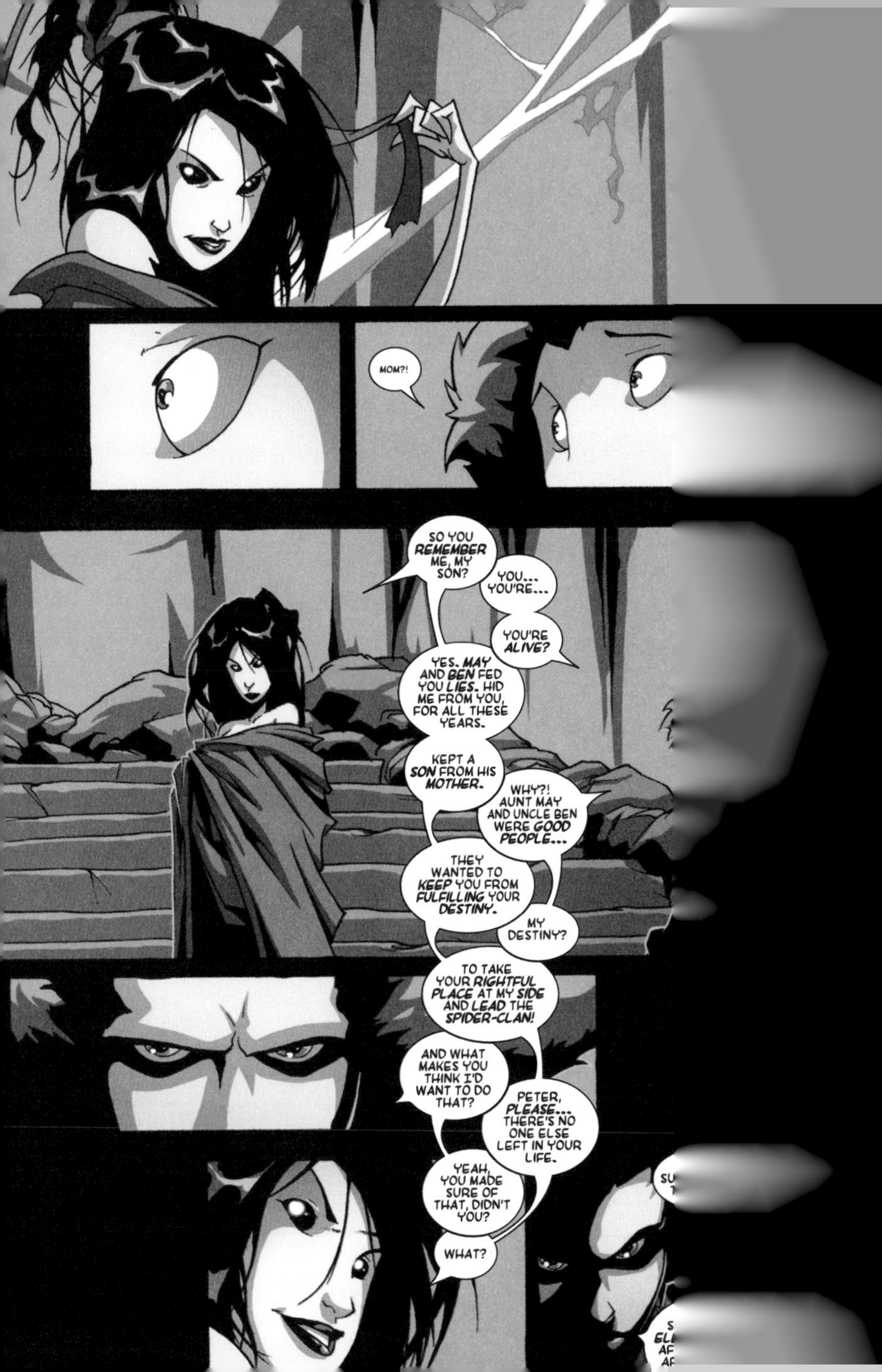
MOM?!
SO YOU REMEMBER ME, MY SON?
YOU... YOU'RE...
YOU'RE ALIVE?
YES. MAY AND BEN FED YOU LIES. HID ME FROM YOU, FOR ALL THESE YEARS.
KEPT A SON FROM HIS MOTHER.
WHY?! AUNT MAY AND UNCLE BEN WERE GOOD PEOPLE...
THEY WANTED TO KEEP YOU FROM FULFILLING YOUR DESTINY.
MY DESTINY?
TO TAKE YOUR RIGHTFUL PLACE AT MY SIDE AND LEAD THE SPIDER-CLAN!
AND WHAT MAKES YOU THINK I'D WANT TO DO THAT?
PETER, PLEASE... THERE'S NO ONE ELSE LEFT IN YOUR LIFE.
YEAH, YOU MADE SURE OF THAT, DIDN'T YOU?
WHAT?

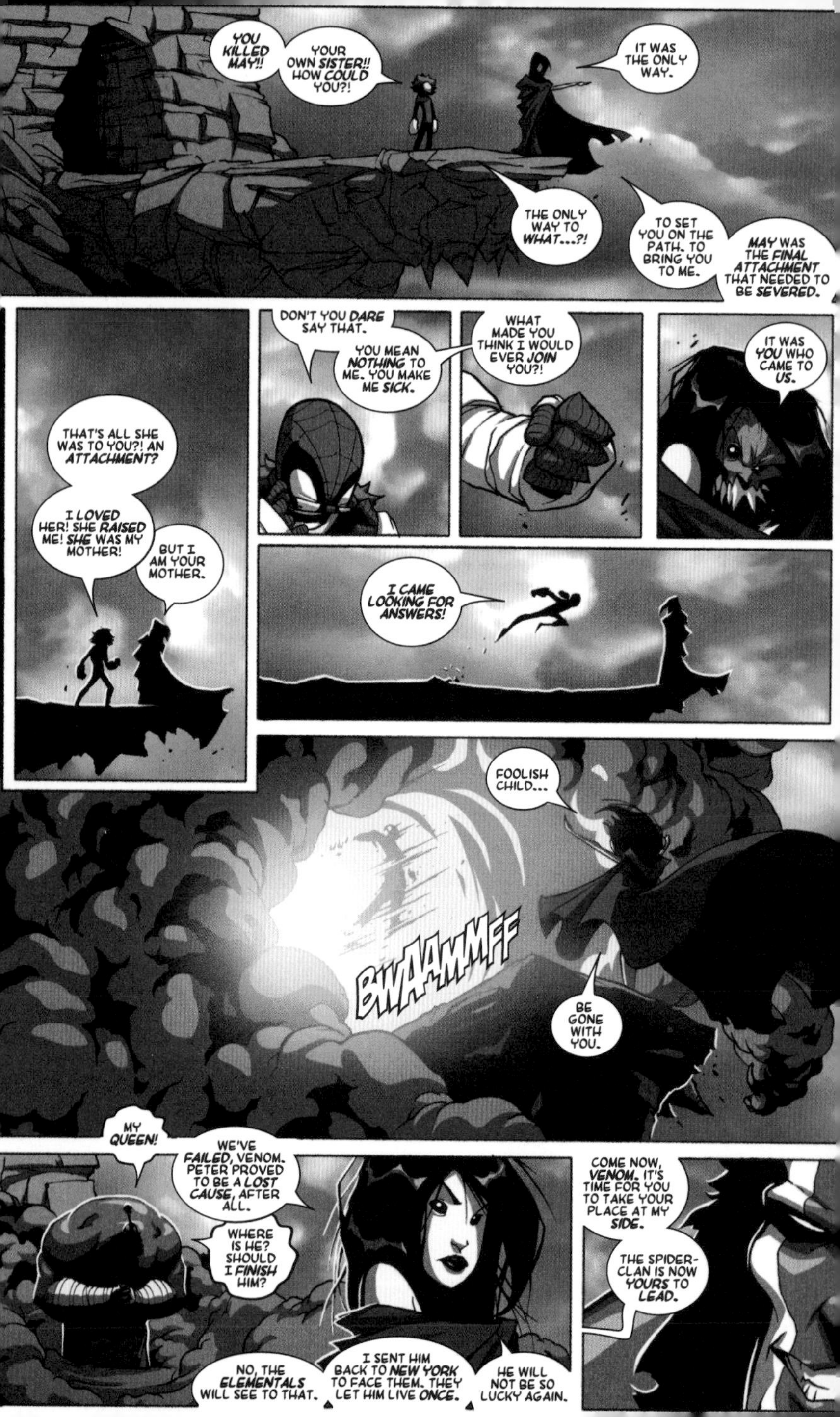
YOU KILLED MAY!!
YOUR OWN SISTER!! HOW COULD YOU?!
IT WAS THE ONLY WAY.
THE ONLY WAY TO WHAT...?!
TO SET YOU ON THE PATH. TO BRING YOU TO ME.
MAY WAS THE FINAL ATTACHMENT THAT NEEDED TO BE SEVERED.
THAT'S ALL SHE WAS TO YOU?! AN ATTACHMENT?
I LOVED HER! SHE RAISED ME! SHE WAS MY MOTHER!
BUT I AM YOUR MOTHER.
DON'T YOU DARE SAY THAT.
YOU MEAN NOTHING TO ME. YOU MAKE ME SICK.
WHAT MADE YOU THINK I WOULD EVER JOIN YOU?!
IT WAS YOU WHO CAME TO US.
I CAME LOOKING FOR ANSWERS!
FOOLISH CHILD...
BWAAMMFF
BE GONE WITH YOU.
MY QUEEN!
WE'VE FAILED, VENOM. PETER PROVED TO BE A LOST CAUSE, AFTER ALL.
WHERE IS HE? SHOULD I FINISH HIM?
NO, THE ELEMENTALS WILL SEE TO THAT.
I SENT HIM BACK TO NEW YORK TO FACE THEM. THEY LET HIM LIVE ONCE.
HE WILL NOT BE SO LUCKY AGAIN.
COME NOW, VENOM. IT'S TIME FOR YOU TO TAKE YOUR PLACE AT MY SIDE.
THE SPIDER-CLAN IS NOW YOURS TO LEAD.

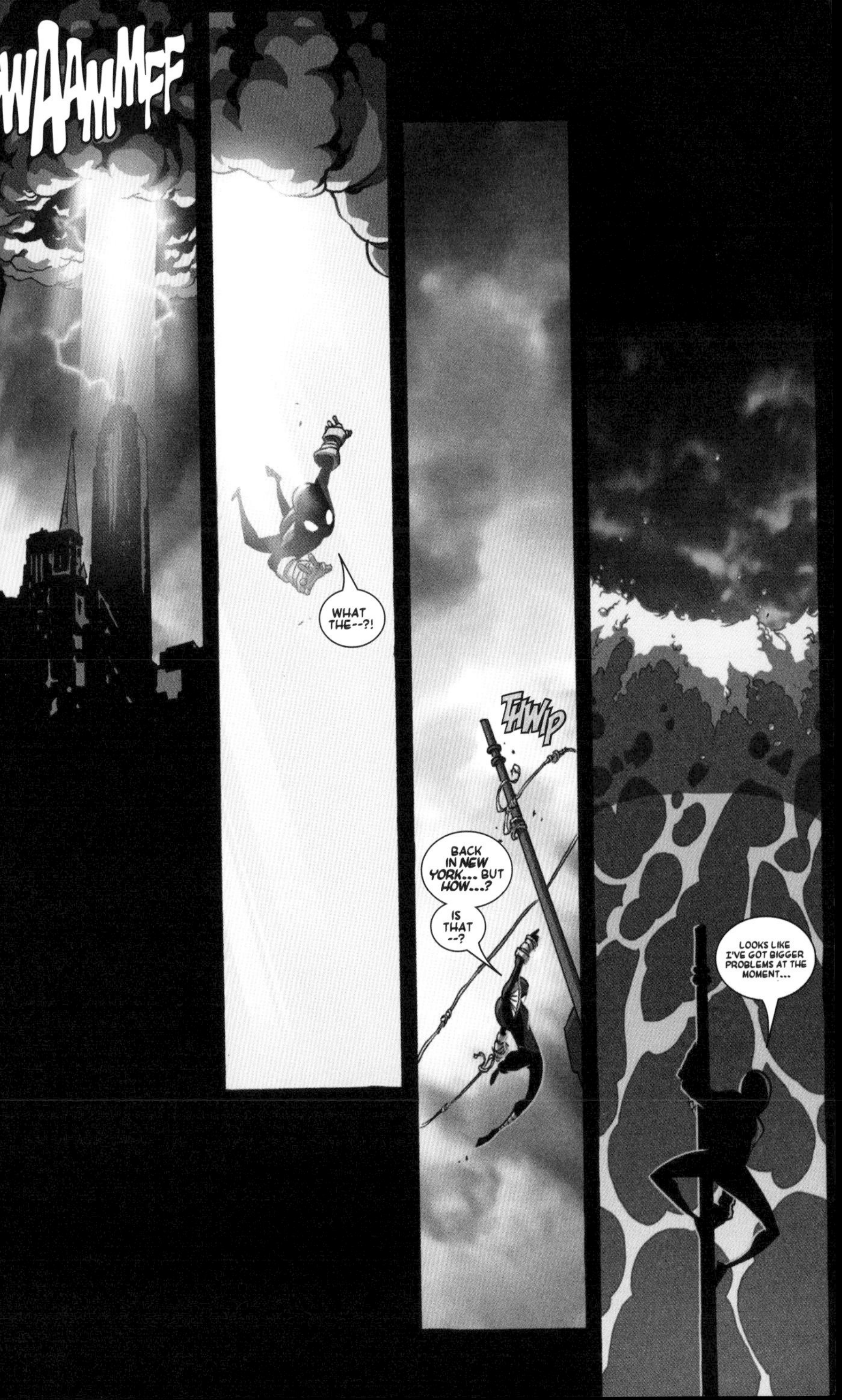

WAAMMFF
WHAT THE--?!
THWIP
BACK IN NEW YORK... BUT HOW...?
IS THAT --?
LOOKS LIKE I'VE GOT BIGGER PROBLEMS AT THE MOMENT...

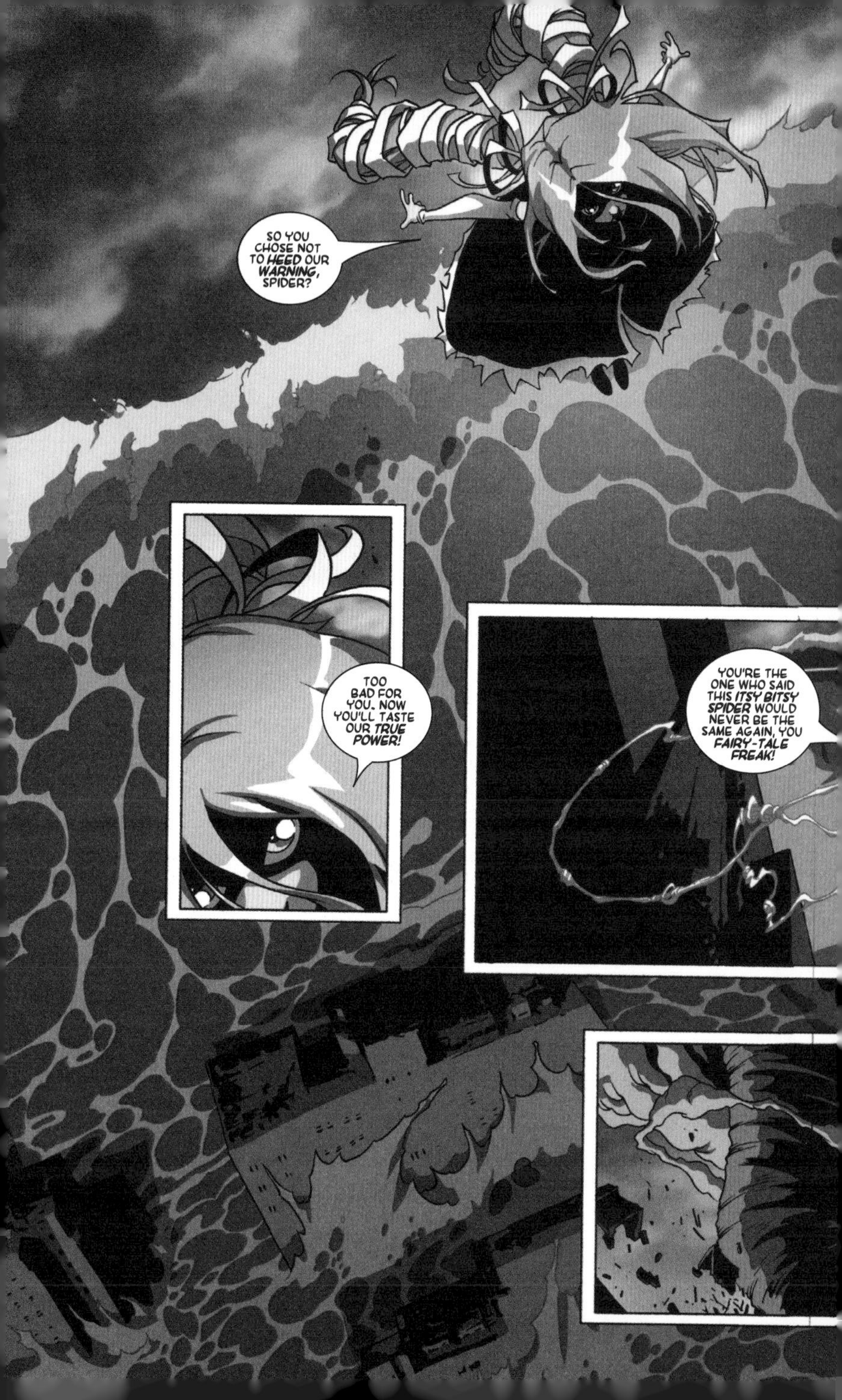
SO YOU CHOSE NOT TO HEED OUR WARNING, SPIDER?
TOO BAD FOR YOU. NOW YOU'LL TASTE OUR TRUE POWER!
YOU'RE THE ONE WHO SAID THIS ITSY BITSY SPIDER WOULD NEVER BE THE SAME AGAIN, YOU FAIRY-TALE FREAK!

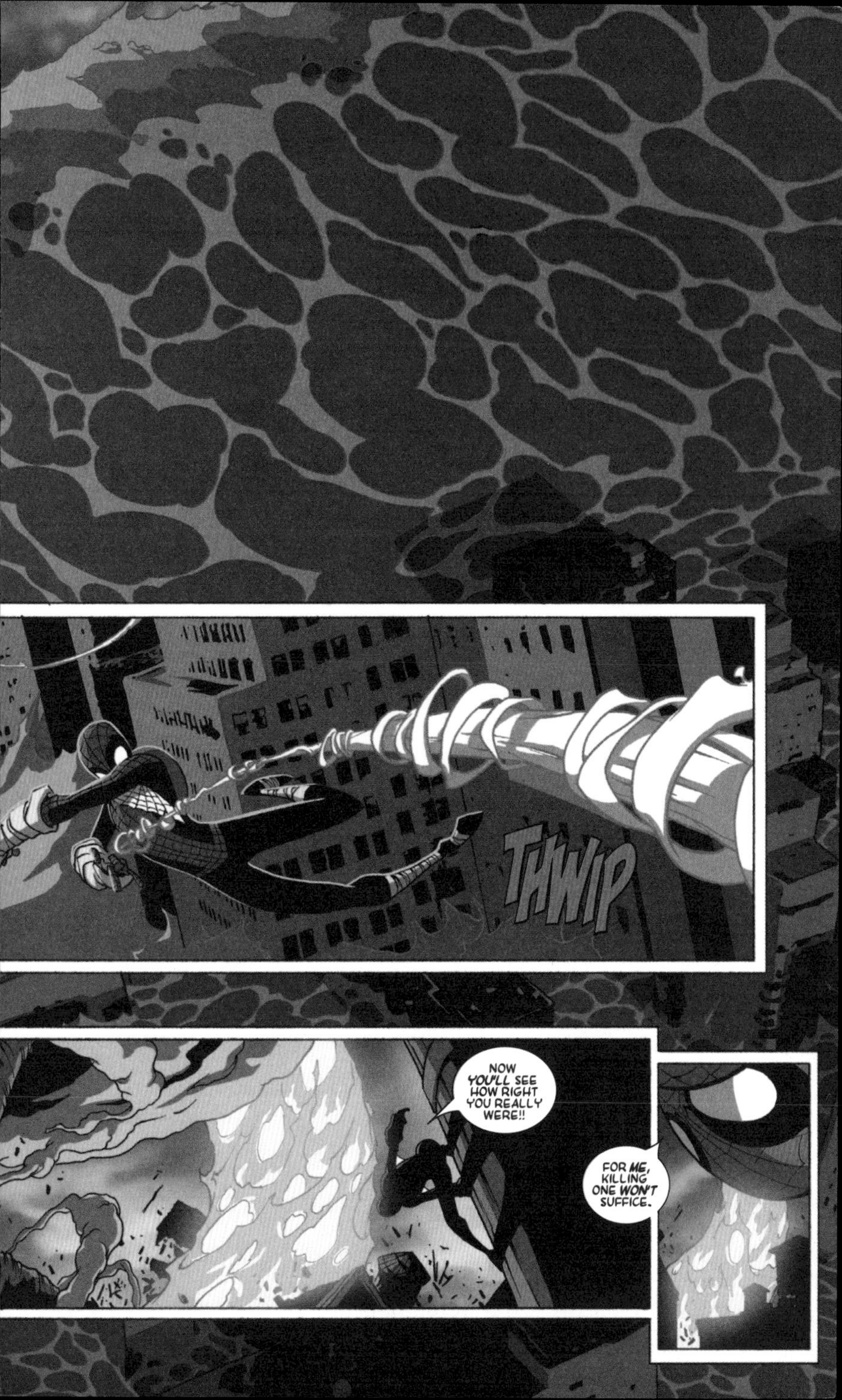
THWIP
NOW YOU'LL SEE HOW RIGHT YOU REALLY WERE!!
FOR ME, KILLING ONE WON'T SUFFICE.

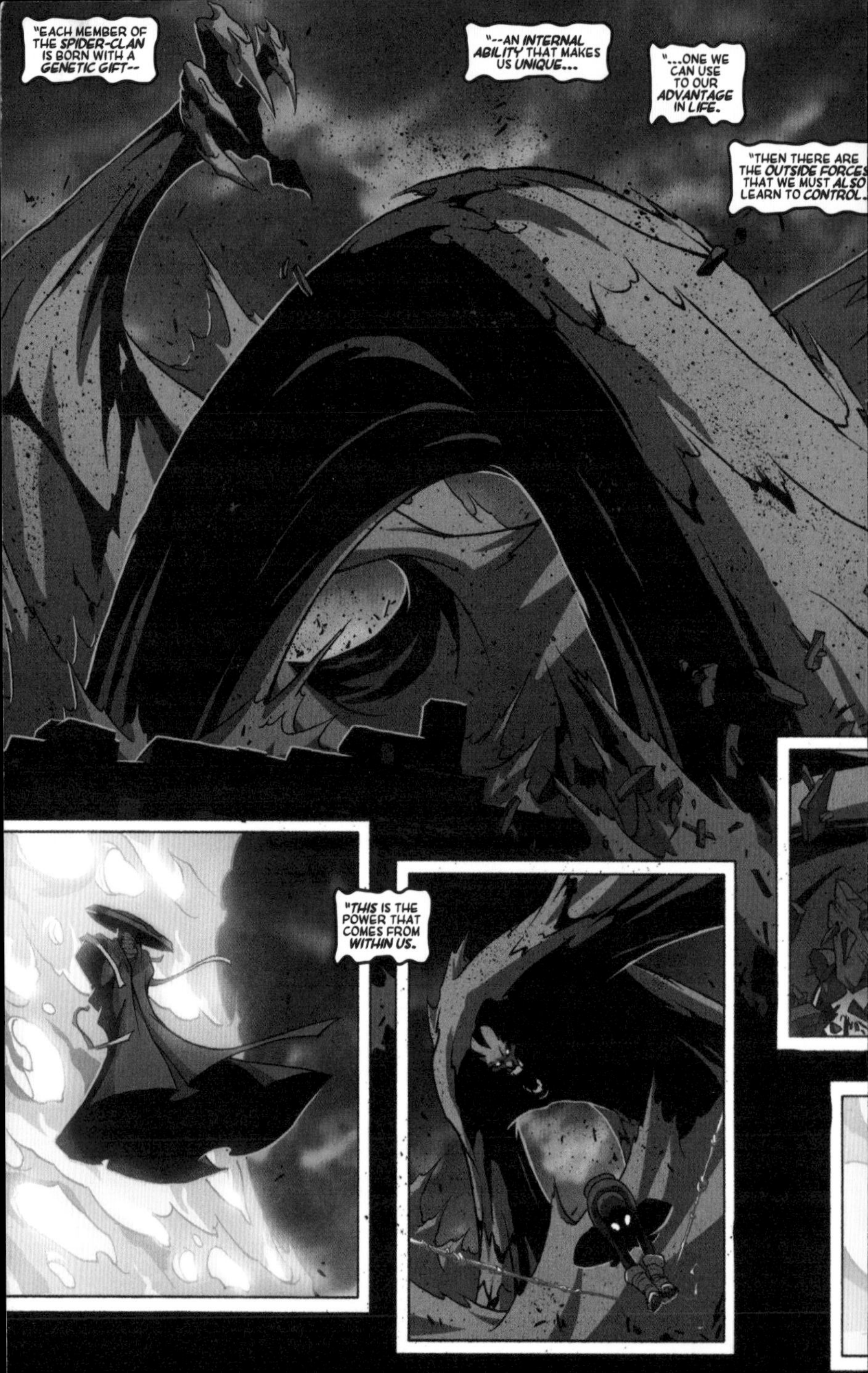
"EACH MEMBER OF THE SPIDER-CLAN IS BORN WITH A GENETIC GIFT--
"--AN INTERNAL ABILITY THAT MAKES US UNIQUE...
"...ONE WE CAN USE TO OUR ADVANTAGE IN LIFE.
"THEN THERE ARE THE OUTSIDE FORCES THAT WE MUST ALSO LEARN TO CONTROL.
"THIS IS THE POWER THAT COMES FROM WITHIN US.

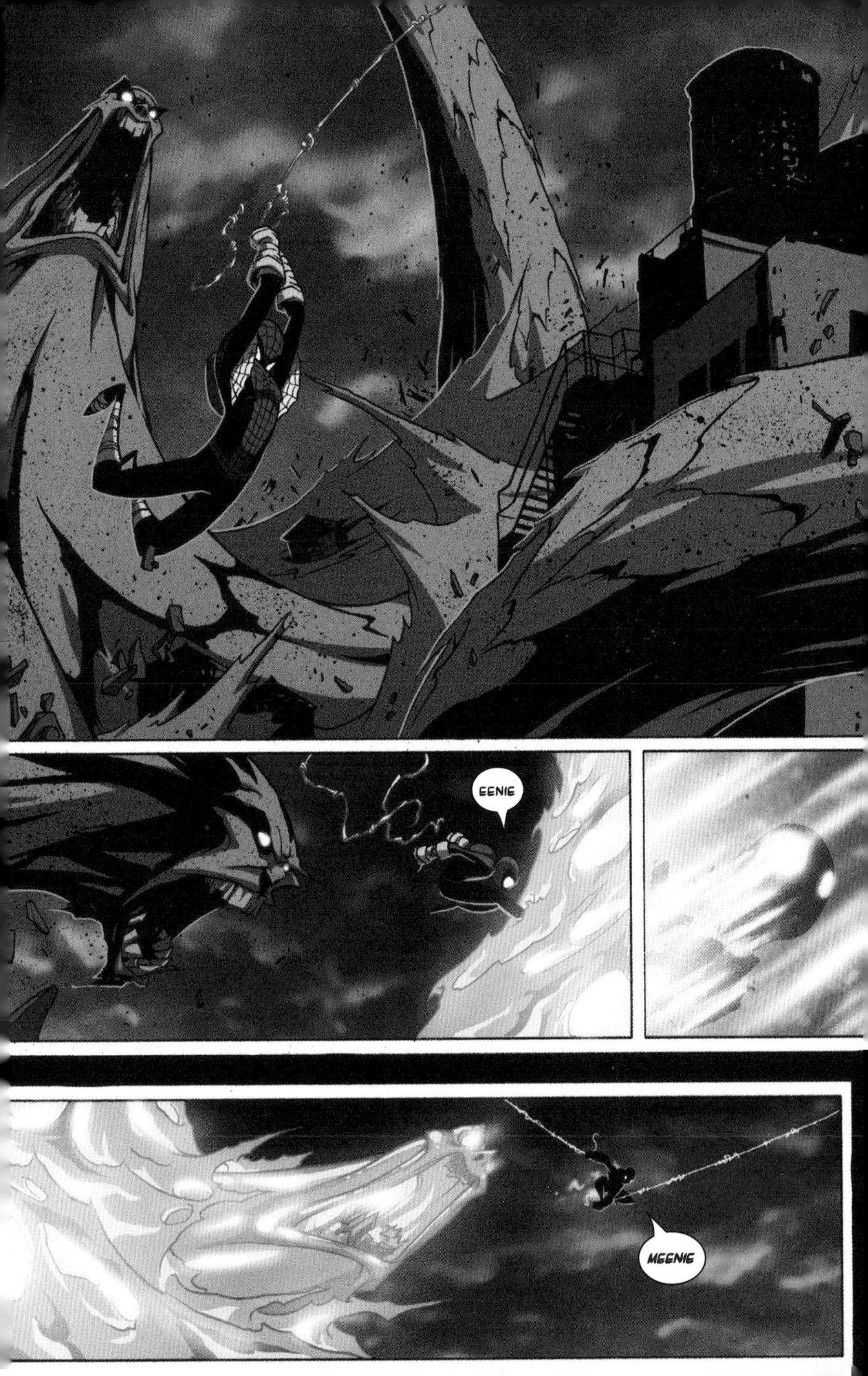
EENIE
MEENIE

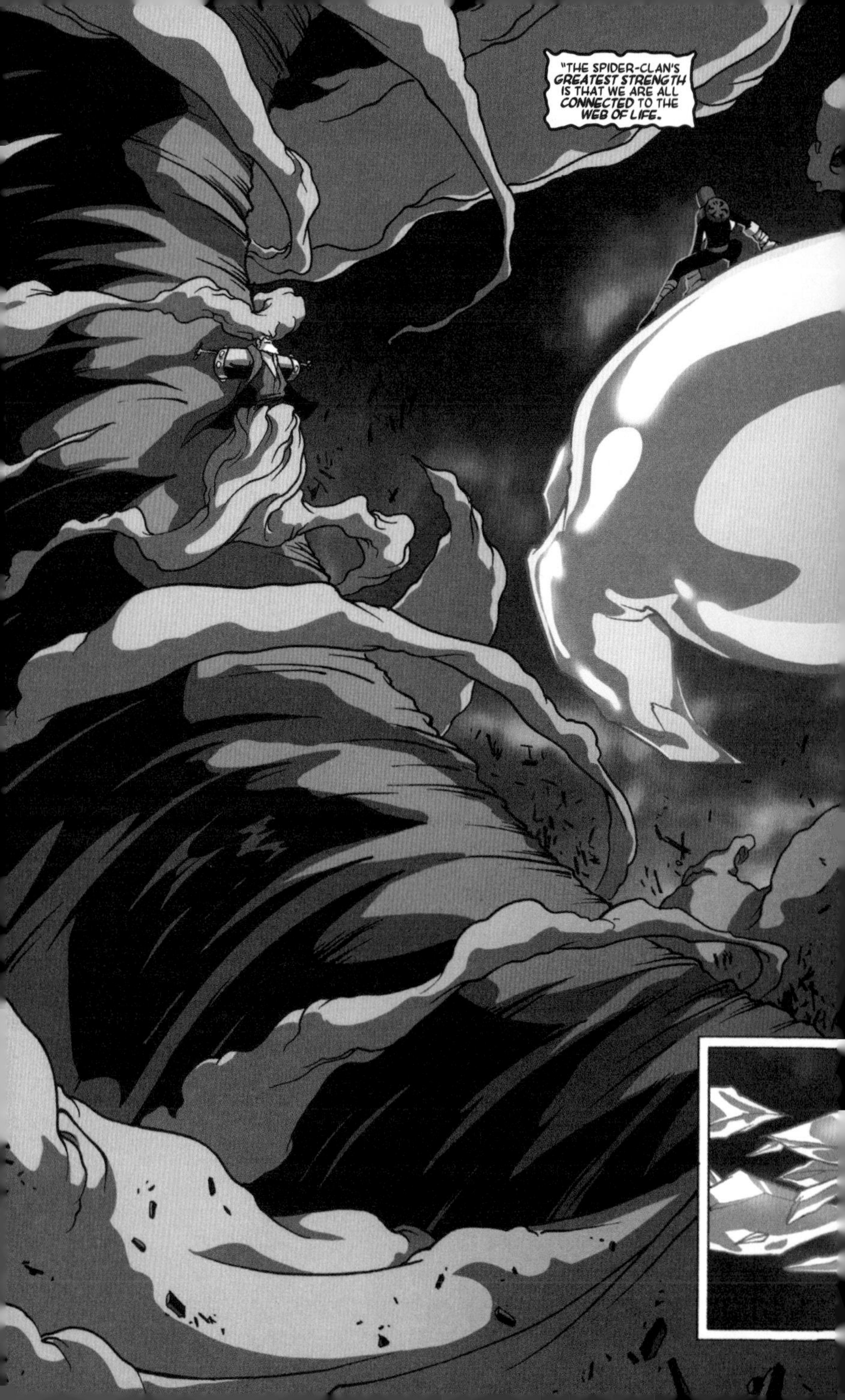
"THE SPIDER-CLAN'S GREATEST STRENGTH IS THAT WE ARE ALL CONNECTED TO THE WEB OF LIFE.

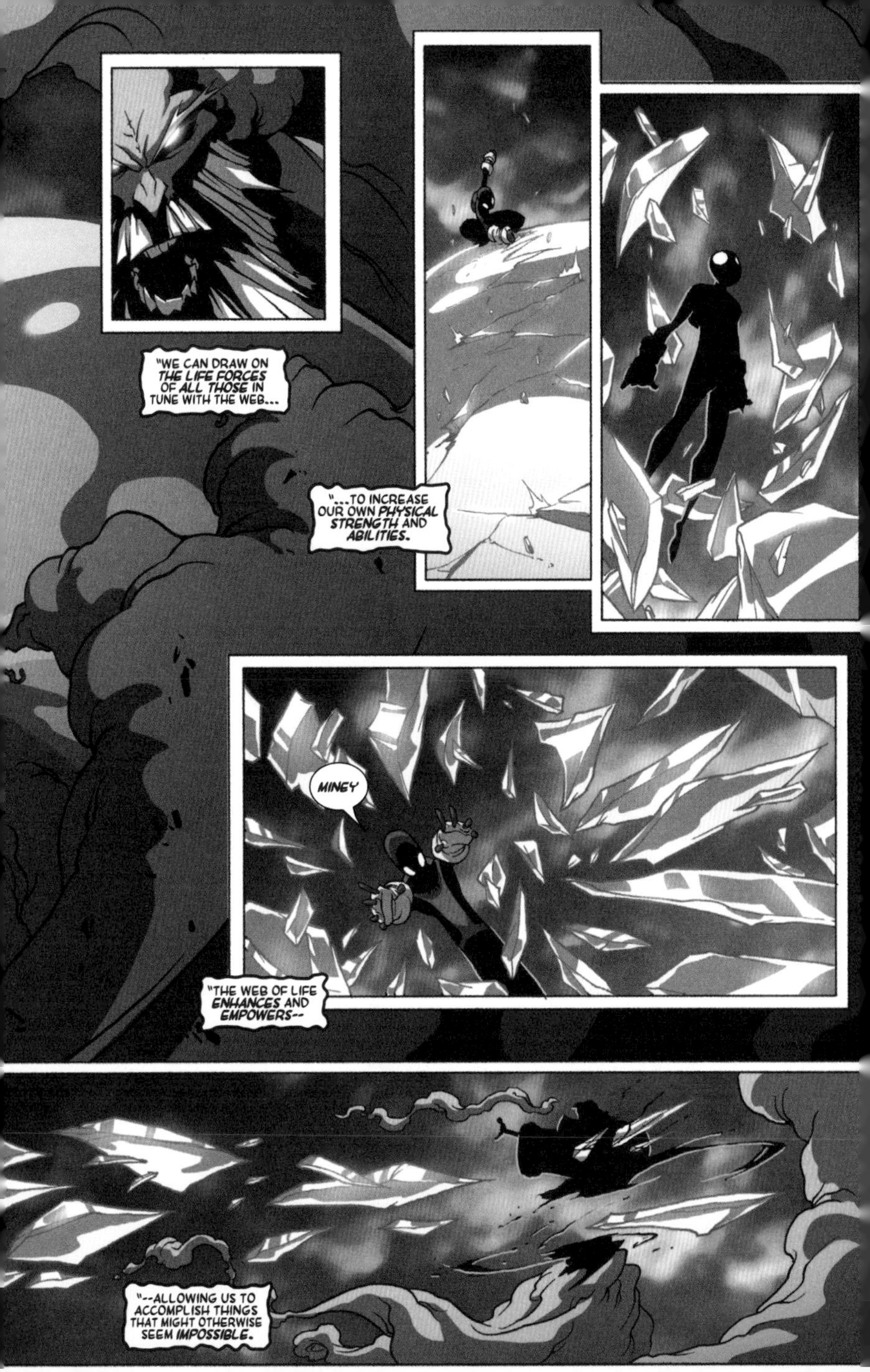

"WE CAN DRAW ON THE LIFE FORCES OF ALL THOSE IN TUNE WITH THE WEB...
"...TO INCREASE OUR OWN PHYSICAL STRENGTH AND ABILITIES.
MINEY
"THE WEB OF LIFE ENHANCES AND EMPOWERS--
"--ALLOWING US TO ACCOMPLISH THINGS THAT MIGHT OTHERWISE SEEM IMPOSSIBLE.

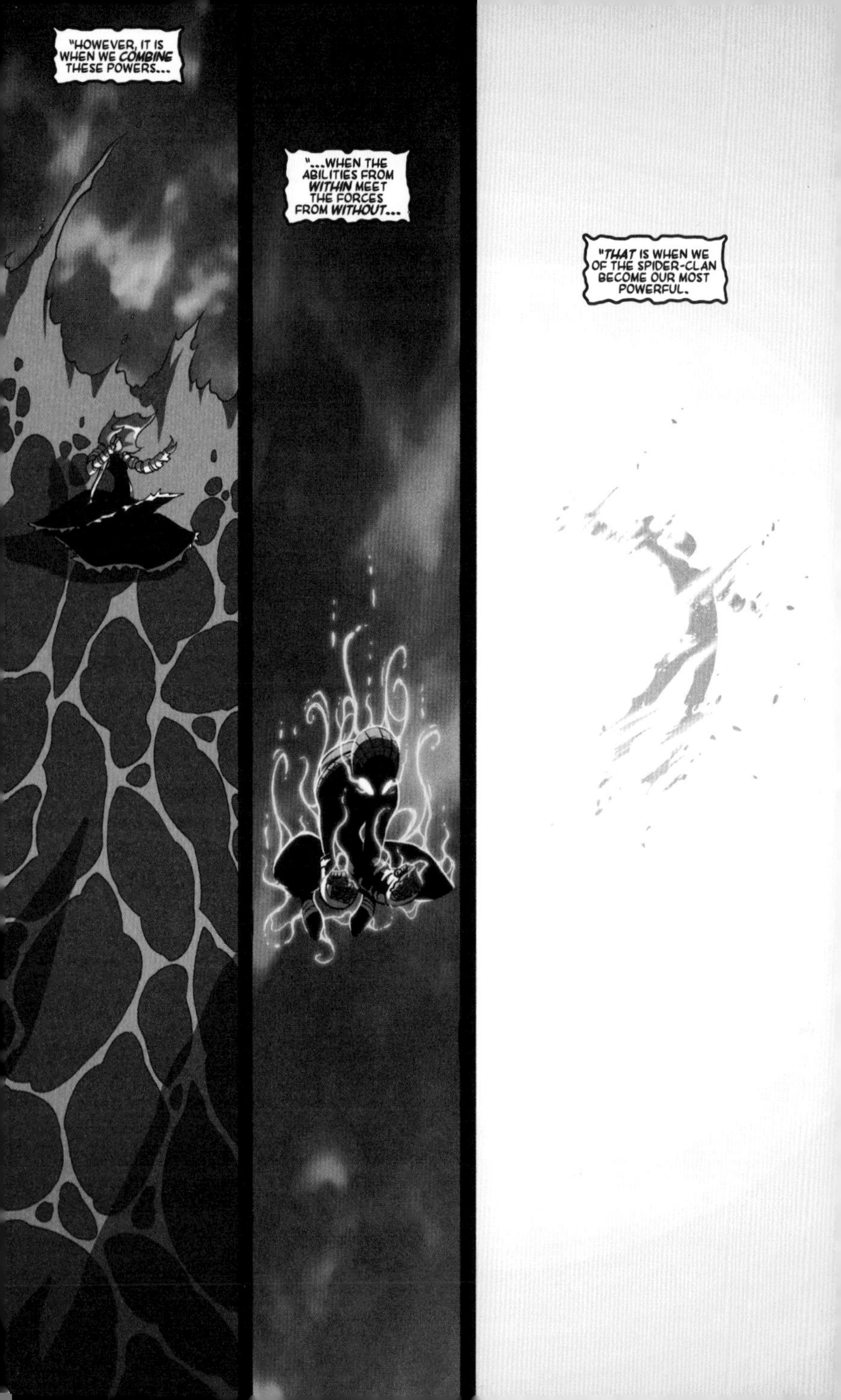
"HOWEVER, IT IS WHEN WE COMBINE THESE POWERS...
"...WHEN THE ABILITIES FROM WITHIN MEET THE FORCES FROM WITHOUT...
"THAT IS WHEN WE OF THE SPIDER-CLAN BECOME OUR MOST POWERFUL.

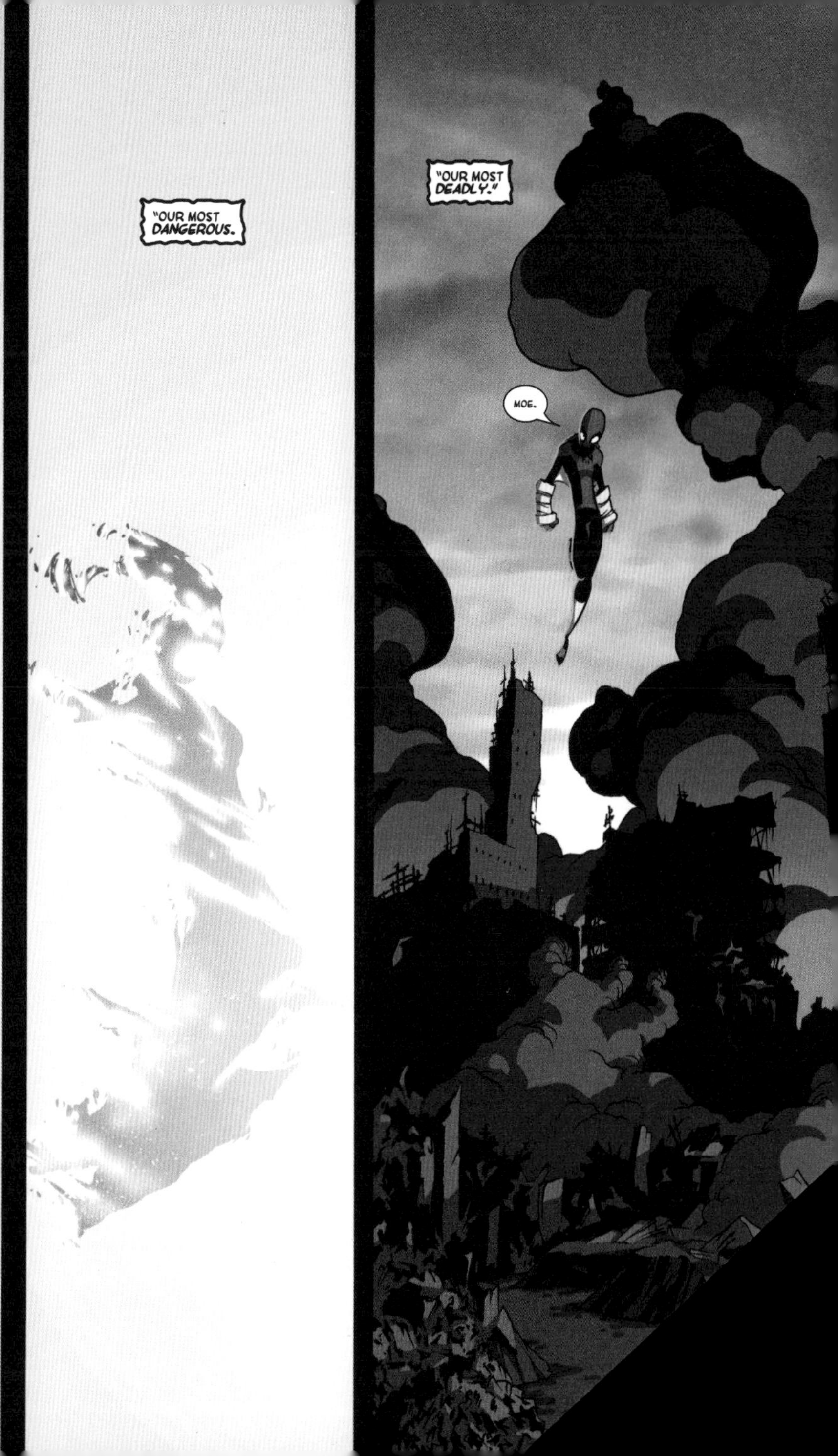
"OUR MOST DANGEROUS.
"OUR MOST DEADLY."
MOE.

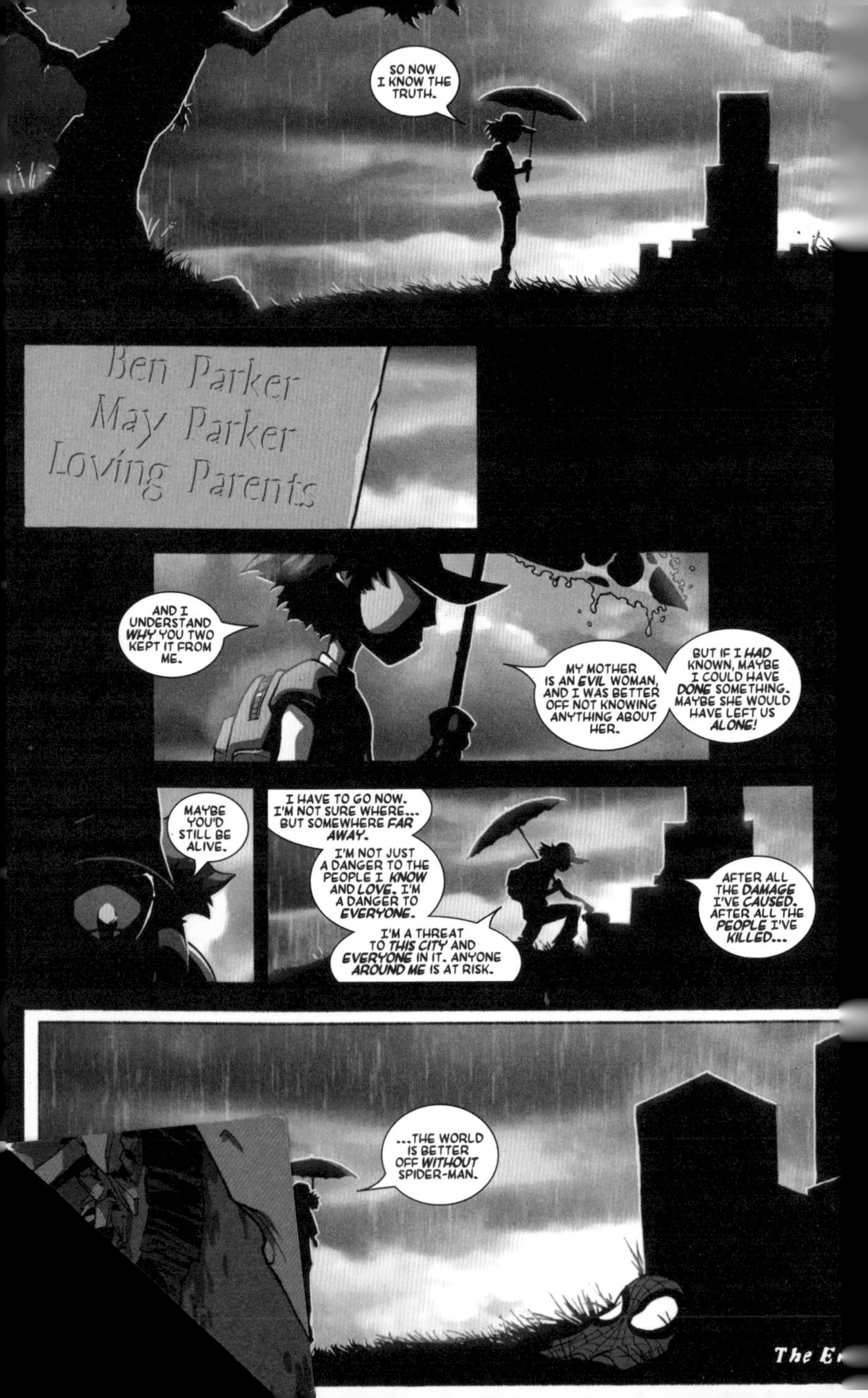
SO NOW I KNOW THE TRUTH.
Ben Parker May Parker Loving Parents
AND I UNDERSTAND WHY YOU TWO KEPT IT FROM ME.
MY MOTHER IS AN EVIL WOMAN, AND I WAS BETTER OFF NOT KNOWING ANYTHING ABOUT HER.
BUT IF I HAD KNOWN, MAYBE I COULD HAVE DONE SOMETHING. MAYBE SHE WOULD HAVE LEFT US ALONE!
MAYBE YOU'D STILL BE ALIVE.
I HAVE TO GO NOW. I'M NOT SURE WHERE... BUT SOMEWHERE FAR AWAY.
I'M NOT JUST A DANGER TO THE PEOPLE I KNOW AND LOVE. I'M A DANGER TO EVERYONE.
I'M A THREAT TO THIS CITY AND EVERYONE IN IT. ANYONE AROUND ME IS AT RISK.
AFTER ALL THE DAMAGE I'VE CAUSED. AFTER ALL THE PEOPLE I'VE KILLED...
...THE WORLD IS BETTER OFF WITHOUT SPIDER-MAN.
The E